I'M NOT IN SALES...I'M A LAWYER!

Grow Your Practice with a Business Development Mindset

R. C. "BOB" GREENE &
VINCENT D. BURRUANO

Vince Burruano Consulting Services, LLC
www.practical-sales-wisdom.com
South Carolina, USA

RCG Workgroup
www.rcgworkgroup.com
Virginia, USA

Robert C. Greene and Vincent D. Burruano
I'M NOT IN SALES…I'M A LAWYER! Grow Your Practice with a Business Development Mindset

eBook ISBN 978-1-7377703-4-3
Paperback ISBN 978-1-7377703-5-0

Nonfiction | Law | General
Nonfiction | Business & Economics | Development | Business Development

DEDICATION

I would like to dedicate this book to my family who provide constant support and encouragement for all my endeavors. I am extremely grateful to have you in my life.

- Vince

I dedicate this book to the memory of my dad, Lee Greene, whose love and respect for the written word inspired my own writing and teaching. And to my dear wife, Irma, whose unwavering support, and belief in me have been a constant source of strength and motivation. And finally, I dedicate this book to every lawyer who aspires to develop a business mindset that can propel their legal practice to new heights.

- Bob

TABLE OF CONTENTS

FOREWORD

As an attorney with over 30 years of practice, I have witnessed the change in the landscape of attorney-client relationships and client development over time. Gone are the days of the long lunches, company holiday parties, and regular in-person meet-and-greet opportunities at a client's physical location during seminars or team meetings. The pandemic rapidly brought even more changes: remote work, turnover of personnel, shortened attention spans, and virtual everything, from meetings to depositions to mediations and even trials. In this virtual world, development of relationships with existing clients and generation of new relationships have gotten much harder. What does this mean? Attorneys must seize every opportunity to sell themselves, and their firms, to the maximum effect.

This book is all about how to accomplish these tasks: learning techniques that make a lasting impression and open the door to the next opportunity.

Bob Greene and Vince Burruano are well equipped to provide these tools, having both been in sales for years, leading teams of sales professionals to optimize sales activities, operations, and strategic marketing. I know Vince personally and have witnessed him successfully wielding the tools outlined in this book to draw people out and develop connections, leading to lasting relationships and business opportunities. Vince and Bob understand that many attorneys believe their work and reputations sell themselves, but in a day of ever-changing personnel, company structures, and work environment, they also understand more is needed. We, as attorneys, need to listen, engage, and connect to build our practices and develop our businesses. This book is an excellent way to learn how.

Dawn E. Boyce, McGavin, Boyce, Bardot, Thorsen & Katz, P.C.

SECTION 1: OPENING STATEMENT

"People will come to you way faster and stay longer to learn something [of value to them] than they will ever come just to be sold to."

Chet Holmes, American business coach and sales and marketing expert

This book is for an attorney, someone like you, who now finds yourself responsible for revenue generation even though you do not have the word "sales" in your job title. If you are responsible for helping to grow and maintain your firm's practice, guess what? You are in sales. And, despite your belief to the contrary, you will now need to develop a business development mindset to be successful.

Unfortunately, most law schools do not include business development techniques in their curriculum. This means that if you graduate from one of these schools and are looking to join a firm, or you are a new associate, you may have not received any formal training on how to attract, maintain, and cultivate a client base. This is unfortunate since this is now considered an essential skill at most firms. Because every lawyer is responsible for attracting clients, law school graduates would be better served if their schools would provide them with some real-world business development tools.

Even if there are professional business development or marketing associates on your firm's staff, you are the best representative to demonstrate the advantages which only you can offer to your clients. This is a personalized service, and someone is hiring you as much as they are retaining your firm. You will have to learn to market yourself to attract the best clients.

Further, promoting your services will provide you with a competitive advantage over other attorneys. Attracting new clients and retaining and growing existing client relationships is a highly desirable skill. Being engaged and demonstrating your commitment to this important activity will allow the senior partners in your firm to take notice and reward your results.

Now to be clear, when we talk about having a business development mindset, we are not talking about marketing or advertising. Those are different skill sets. For us, having a business development mindset is how to engage with prospective clients to understand their needs so they can see the value in working with you to help solve their problems. If you happen to be a litigator, you will also need to be able to "sell" your story to a judge, jury, or other attorneys. To the degree we sell ourselves and our ideas, we are all in sales.

Sidebar: The Power of a Story

Before the written word, stories were how information was passed from one person to the next. Storytelling is a key component of our shared history, and it remains one of the most effective ways to convey information to people today. People find it easier to learn from a story and often remember the details much better.[1]

Most good stories have the same basic narrative structure. It can be broken down into six ideas that you can use to tell your story too.

1. Once upon a time…there were people in need of legal services who did not know how to find an attorney they could trust.
2. Every day…they would scour the internet looking at reviews and ratings, which were not always reliable.
3. One day…I decided to stop depending on online reviews to steer clients to me and I started meeting people in the community at their events.
4. Because of that…they got to know me and the services I can offer through my firm.

---

[1] Boris, V. (2017, Dec. 20). *Leading the Way: What Makes Storytelling So Effective For Learning? Harvard Business Publishing Corporate Learning.* Retrieved from https://www.harvardbusiness.org/what-makes-storytelling-so-effective-for-learning/

5. Because of that…I became someone they know and trust to help them when they need legal services.
6. Until finally…they became my clients and are now referring people to me so those people no longer need to rely on the internet to find an attorney they can trust.

Develop a repertoire of appropriate stories to have ready when needed. When you are new, it may be difficult to find stories in which you have been directly involved. That is fine. You can use stories from other attorneys on your team as a basis for developing your own story library. Instead of saying, "I have a client who…" you can say something like, "My associate worked with a client in a very similar situation, and we were able to help provide a solution that exceeded their expectations." The client is interested in solving their problem or gaining an advantage, and a compelling story can help them better understand how you and your firm can help them achieve those goals.

A good best practice is to create a 'story book' to capture the important details of both your successes and your company's successes in helping people. While you wouldn't give this book to a prospective client, the value is in helping you organize the various stories you may want to share. Depending on your practice, you will want to have a story for each of the services you offer. Also consider the types of clients you have assisted. For example, perhaps you specialize in three or four vertical markets (healthcare, professional services, or finance). It would be more powerful to have a story for each service for each market category. This will help you convey the most appropriate story for maximum impact. The more specific you can be about the initial situation (the problem) and how that problem was impacting the client's business (the business implication), the more powerful your explanation of how your firm was able to help them (the solution). Remember, if the only tool you know how to use is a hammer, then everything will look like a nail. Build your toolbox to be prepared to handle all manner of screws, bolts, and fasteners.

There's also science behind good storytelling. After a presentation, only 5% of prospects remember statistics, but 63% will remember stories.[2] As mentioned above, as listeners, we're hardwired to be pulled into good stories: "When we hear a story, the neural activity [in our brains]

---

[2] Carlon Rush, B. (2014, Aug. 28). *Science of storytelling: why and how to use it in your marketing*. The Guardian. Retrieved November 16, 2022 from https://www.theguardian.com/media-network/media-network-blog/2014/aug/28/science-storytelling-digital-marketing

increases fivefold–like a switchboard has suddenly illuminated the city of our mind."[3] Scientists like to say that "Neurons that fire together, wire together."[4] When more of your brain is engaged at a given point of time, the chances that your brain will remember a story increases exponentially.

One of the reasons for this is that our brains react to stories we hear in the same way they do when we actually do things. There is no differentiation. What this means is that when we listen to a story, our brain will react as if we are actively part of the story. Using metaphors when telling stories is a highly effective way to help people experience a story as if they were living it themselves. When telling stories, also infuse facts into your narrative to appeal to both emotion and logic.

Further when hearing a story, our brain will be on alert to decipher what it hears. This is a primitive response to

---

[3] Bonomo, L. (2018, May 10). *"When we hear a story, the neural activity increases fivefold--like a switchboard has suddenly illuminated the city of our mind"*. LinkedIn. Retrieved November 16, 2022 from https://www.linkedin.com/pulse/when-we-hear-story-neural-activity-increases-has-suddenly-bonomo/?articleId=6400309692098183168

[4] Samadi, A. (2017, May 17). *Neurons that Fire Together Wire Together, So Simple!* LinkedIn. Retrieved November 16, 2022 from https://www.linkedin.com/pulse/neurons-fire-together-wire-so-simple-andrea-samadi/

outside stress that is stimulated by a hormone called cortisol. Responsible for our "fight or flight" response, the release of cortisol gets us to pay attention to our surroundings and to a story being told.[5] If the story is amusing and makes us smile, our brain will release the "feel-good" hormone, dopamine. As a neurotransmitter associated with pleasurable sensations, dopamine puts us at ease and allows us to focus on the story without feeling stressed or anxious.[6] Because we are in a "happy" place, we also will most likely feel more engaged.

As neuroeconomics pioneer Paul Zak discovered, stories that are highly engaging can elicit powerful empathic responses by triggering a neurochemical called oxytocin. Oxytocin is often referred to as the "trust hormone." This neurochemical promotes connection and encourages people to feel empathy. When released in the brain of your prospective client, oxytocin can help you

---

[5] Smith, J.A. (2016, Aug. 25). *The science of the story.* Berkeley News, UC Berkeley. Retrieved November 16, 2022, from https://news.berkeley.edu/berkeley_blog/the-science-of-the-story/

[6] Trafton, A. (2018, Nov. 7). *Dopamine primes the brain for enhanced vigilance: Neuroscientists discover a circuit that helps redirect attention to focus on potential threats.* MIT News, Massachusetts Institute of Technology. Retrieved November 16, 2022, from https://news.mit.edu/2018/dopamine-brain-vigilance-anxiety-1107

to build trust in your law firm and you as a lawyer, and in doing so, open up the possibility of you acquiring a new client.

You see, when you tell a story from the perspective of having a mindset for business development, we help the subconscious mind of our prospect to truly "get" and see the benefit of our legal services and to decide where they are of most value. Make your stories honest, authentic, and truthful. Andrew Davis said, "Content builds relationships. Relationships are built on trust. Trust drives revenue." For your next client meeting, tell a good story.

Our intention is for this book to provide you with a functional overview of what it looks like to have a business development mindset. It will help you to understand what skills are necessary to become effective at creating new client relationships, retaining current clients, and increasing revenue from your existing clientele. It is not intended to make you a "salesperson." Rather, it is designed to help you develop a positive mindset about promoting yourself in a respectable, professional, and compelling manner.

We have designed this book to be a starting point for your journey to become a rainmaker. In addition to discussing the key concepts, we have included a 30-day plan that will help you organize your efforts and develop a cadence to help you put what we will teach you to work. We also provide you with additional information, examples, and templates that are available on our website at http://www.imnotinsales.com. You can also contact us there for any specific questions you may have. We are happy and ready to assist you. We are available to provide individual coaching sessions. Contact us at http://www.imnotinsales.com for more information.

To give you a broad-based perspective, we will be supplementing our own proven sales expertise with additional insights from other authors and business development experts so you can align yourself with the approach that is most comfortable and effective for you.

Just like you have already made the commitment to your profession to stay current on new rules, regulations, and case law, there are new tools and strategies that are continuously emerging for business development you need to understand as well.

While attracting clients is not easy, it is essential. The concept, at first glance, appears to be simple, but mastery takes an ongoing commitment and years of diligent practice. The good news is that business development is a learnable skill. In this book, our focus is to help you achieve a business development mindset, so you better understand and appreciate what it takes to sell your ideas and yourself to prospective clients. We will challenge you to think in new ways to better monetize your time, not just your billable hours. The benefits are significant, and this investment of your attention is worth the effort.

Rest assured, we have worked with countless other professionals just like you and we have helped them achieve a business development mindset to grow their practice too.

Now, let's get started!

I'm Not in Sales!

CHAPTER 1: THIS WASN'T TAUGHT IN LAW SCHOOL

"We are all in the business of sales."

Dave Ramsey, American personal finance personality

We completely appreciate your situation. You went to college and then law school. You worked hard to pass the bar and to become a lawyer. You were able to secure an associate position with a law firm and you are poised for growth, advancement, and all the trappings that come with a successful legal career. You are working long hours to put forth your best efforts on even the most mundane tasks to demonstrate your value and readiness to tackle any undertaking. You are a model associate catching the eye of the heavy hitters in your firm potentially on the fast track to your first promotion.

Then someone, probably the managing partner, walked into your office and said, in addition to the splendid work you are currently doing, you will also need to start developing your own client base. "We need you to go out there to cultivate and secure additional new business for the firm." Congratulations. Despite not having the word sales in your job title, you have now entered the rewarding and challenging world of business development. However, in your head you are thinking, "Excuse me, I'm a lawyer! I'm not a salesperson." As you wrap your mind around this new responsibility and endeavor to comprehend the meaning of what you are hearing, you fight back your initial reaction to say, "You must be freaking kidding me! If I had wanted to go into sales, I would not have become a lawyer. I would have skipped all the extra years of school, and the corresponding student loans, and went out to sell widgets door to door or used cars in a big plaid jacket. What is going on here?"

The truth is that today everyone is in sales. Nothing in this world happens until somebody sells something. No matter who you are or what you do professionally, we all need to have a sales mindset. And if you think about it, you have a lot of experience already. Just recall your childhood. You were an expert in getting what you wanted. How many times did you take "no" for a final answer? Never. You kept asking again and again until you either got what you wanted or went on to ask for the next thing that you wanted. This is a very rudimentary picture of the tenacity that a business development mindset requires and a skill which, to a certain degree, you already possess. We just need to refine the approach so that it better aligns to your profession. Just like when you were a child and you didn't always get what you asked for, as an adult you are not always successful in getting everything you want either. However, as a child, if you didn't get what you wanted, you simply asked for something else. You were never deterred by asking for a ride to the local video game store or a bowl of ice cream. It's the same idea now that you are an adult. A negative answer now should not discourage you from starting the process over the next time there is something that you want, which in this case could be a new client or more work from an existing one. So, pat yourself on the back for the grit and tenacity of your youth. You have already taken the first steps toward achieving a sales mindset…and you did not even realize it.

Let us face the facts. If you are not cultivating and securing new clients, your phenomenal legal mind alone will probably not get you the proverbial "corner office" you covet and the accompanying prestige. Instead, it will end up going to some mediocre attorney who struggles to compose a decent brief but who does a fantastic job of bringing new clients to the firm. After all, it is the fee-paying clients who help generate the bonus pool that the partners share at the end of the year. Despite your best work, you will not benefit as readily as the associate who is able to bring new clients into the firm. Is this fair? Maybe not. But is this reality? Absolutely.

Today, law firms are developing specific financial goals in order for associates to progress to the next level in their career. It is no longer just about your legal abilities, but your ability to generate business through the onboarding of new clients or increased billing from existing clients. They may also set the bar for an increasing amount of revenue each year and include revenue generation as a requirement benchmark to progress towards partnership. It is essential to remember that new clients are the lifeblood of any business enterprise including law firms.

If you want to advance in your career, you should consider embracing a business development mindset that will allow you to contribute to the firm as not only an effective attorney, but also as a great business developer. Think of the possibilities and opportunities for continued success. This book is the starting place for your journey. We will show you the way.

If you are still trying to come to grips with your situation, perhaps some sage advice from Vince's mother, Jeanne, would be appropriate. She would often remind him, when confronted by a difficulty, to just "build a bridge and get over it!" Great advice. Here is the good news. Like we said before, achieving a business development mindset may not be easy, but it is a perspective that can be learned, and even mastered, if you are willing to do the work. Yep, it requires work like most worthy pursuits in life. The sooner you get to it, the sooner you will reap the rewards.

In this book, we will provide you with the basic information you will need to develop a business development mindset to build mutually beneficial client relationships for you and your firm. We will start with the fundamentals and slowly build towards a plan you can execute. We also provide you with some additional content at http://www.imnotinsales.com which you can access to help you on your journey. Finally, we are available to answer any questions you may have. Just submit your questions through the website, and we will respond in a timely manner.

We encourage you to be a student of learning. While this book is an excellent resource, the organizations we recommend also have learning opportunities and guest speakers who can provide additional insights regarding how you can achieve a business development mindset. You should take advantage of these opportunities to incorporate new skills, gain perspective, and sharpen your abilities. Remember, the more proficient you become, the more clients you will secure, and the more your career and compensation will grow.

Every law practice has one thing in common. The need for paying clients to stay in business. Even though some larger firms employ a professional sales and marketing team to locate and convert prospects into clients, most firms expect their associates and partners to do this important work as well. What you need to understand is that marketing, advertising, and public relations are all passive activities insufficient to generate the number of new clients most firms need to grow. Business development, on the other hand, is dynamic, proactive, and engaging. It is the best way we know of, outside of possible hypnosis, to get someone to see your point of view and to agree to retain your firm to represent them. You may even discover that you actually enjoy the business development mindset with a little practice and success.

CHAPTER 2: BECOMING A RAINMAKER

"The purpose of business is to create and keep a customer."

Peter Drucker, Austrian-American management consultant, widely recognized as the "father" of the modern business corporation

We are recommending that you garner a business development mindset to help you monetize your practice. Lawyers who are skilled at bringing on new and high-paying clients are called rainmakers. Being called a rainmaker is a term of endearment used to compliment a lawyer who helps "rain money" into the firm. It is the accolade every attorney covets. It is the gold standard of your success.

Rainmakers are sought after in every industry. They are a special breed who have honed their business development mindset so that they can maximize the return on their business development efforts. In many cases, it may not resemble selling at all. But in fact, it is the highest possible level of selling because rainmakers recognize problems and the way in which they can help people solve those problems. Regarding the law, this enables them to earn trust from their clients and to generate significant sums for their firm and, in turn earn substantial compensation as recognition for the monetization of their business development mindset at an elite level.

Here is a list of key attributes that give us insight into the sales mindset of a rainmaker. As an exercise, take a moment to think about the characteristics you already possess. Then consider how with a little more effort, you can achieve some truly remarkable results.

1. They do not think in terms of fees or revenue, but in terms of building a business through mutually beneficial relationships.

2. They build their business one client at a time, and always leverage the last client into future clients.

3. They listen more than they speak to learn how they can best help their clients.

4. They are willing to invest their time in networking and community activities because they recognize the difference between contact and contract is the "R" which stands for relationship.

5. They are focused, and they invest their time in ways that positively impact their business. They avoid expending energy on things that do not contribute to their success.

6. They do not rely on marketplace economies to determine their outcomes. Instead, they rely on their thoughtful actions to determine their results. In short, they make their own “good luck.”

7. They connect with people regularly, through formalized networking or reconnecting with existing contacts, building mutually-beneficial relationships.

8. They surround themselves with successful people and overachievers while avoiding negative people and detractors.

9. They strive for more than just good enough.

10. They don’t see challenges as problems. Rather, they see challenges as opportunities.

11. They continually invest in their personal and professional development. They recognize there is always something new to learn.

12. They do not rely on others to hold themselves accountable. They intrinsically hold themselves to the highest standards.

13. They are recognized subject matter experts in their fields and become trusted advisors by their clients.

Although not everyone in a law firm will become a rainmaker, every lawyer can develop a positive rainmaker attitude. By that we mean that every lawyer can adopt a business development mindset and better position themselves for improving their new client acquisition efforts. As Vince Lombardi famously said, "We will chase perfection, and we will chase it relentlessly, knowing all the while we can never attain it. But along the way, we shall catch excellence." In that spirit we will chase becoming a rainmaker and along the way significantly increase your client acquisition capabilities.

Extroverts vs. Introverts

There seems to be an incorrect assumption that some people are just naturally good at sales or business development. We do not subscribe to this belief. While there are those with certain attributes that lend themselves to being more effective at business development, we believe that achieving a business development mindset is a skill set that can be learned by anyone willing to make the effort.

That leads us to the brief discussion on extroverts vs. introverts. Again, there are some who believe being an extrovert provides an advantage when networking and engaging others. Afterall, an extrovert is outgoing, gregarious, and loves the spotlight. While there are certainly examples of extroverts who have mastered the business development mindset, there is no reason to believe that an introvert cannot be equally, or even more, effective.

Introverts might actually have an advantage in this regard since they tend to be focused on others. Some may call this having a high emotional quotient (EQ). We call it having a proper business development mindset. When you use your business development mindset, you understand that conversation is not about us. It is never about how important we are, rather, it is about how important we make others feel when we are with them. The ability to listen and demonstrate empathy are important qualities in developing mutually-beneficial relationships. It demonstrates your understanding of people, and how they think, feel, and behave. In this way, introverts may be better positioned to create the intimacy required to make a meaningful connection.

Matthew Pollard, a self-professed introvert who is incredibly successful in sales has written and spoken extensively about introverts and the advantage that they have in selling. We encourage you to review his work including *The Introvert's Edge* to learn more about leveraging your inherent nature to be more successful. In his book, Pollard shares how introvert's can find their natural confidence, prepare for every situation, easily sidestep objections, ask for the sale (without asking), and leverage the power of virtual and social networking. As Pollard said, "Stop waiting for all the lights to be green, believe and start taking action."

But wait, you might feel as if sometimes you're a bit of an extrovert, and sometimes a bit of an introvert. That's okay too. If you have a foot in both camps, you may be an ambivert. Regardless of whether you're an extrovert, introvert, or an ambivert, there is no such thing as an ideal persona for having a business development mindset. Rather, as a lawyer, having a business development mindset is about seeing the world from the perspective of your clients to help them appreciate the benefits of working with you.

Being a Good Lawyer May Not be Enough

In this book, we promote our belief that achieving a business development mindset is a skill that can be learned by anyone. Like any skill it is important to study and work towards that goal. The best approach is to learn the fundamentals and then engage in deliberate practice. Eventually these skills will become habits you can use in real life situations. As learners, we all learn differently. According to the VARK model of learning, there are four primary learning modality preferences: Visual, Auditory, Reading/Writing, and Kinesthetic.[7]

Based on our experience in coaching professionals on how to develop a business development mindset, we strongly recommend the kinesthetic learning process of

---

[7] Vark Learn Limited. (2022). *The VARK Modalities.* VARK: A Guide to Learning Preferences. Retrieved Aug. 25, 2022, from https://vark-learn.com/introduction-to-vark/the-vark-modalities/

learning by doing. Do not wait until you become an "expert." It is far better to learn by doing and commence using these skills as soon as you can. By this we mean that you should learn from every engagement and activity in which you participate. You will find that with time and practice, you will continually refine your approach and language and will become more comfortable and confident. Confidence is a magnet of attraction. And having confidence in communicating how you can help your clients will allow you to further hone your business development mindset and improve the quality of your networking engagements.

A key to achieving the business development mindset is to be purposeful in your activities. This requires you to think proactively. To plan your work and then work your plan. Just like when you construct a legal brief or prepare a defense motion, successful legal professionals are strategic in their approach and invest their time in a thoughtful manner to reap the greatest returns from the effort they invest. We encourage you to have a similar mindset when it comes to business development for your law practice.

We have prepared a sample action plan later in this book to help you schedule time on your calendar to engage in these activities. While you should always be on the lookout for an opportunity to promote your services, you will find that establishing a cadence will help ensure that you dedicate the appropriate amount of time to this effort each day. It will also allow you to best monitor your progress and make the necessary adjustments that may be required to reach your goal. To achieve the desired results, you will need to do the right activities properly and consistently.

Remember, achieving a business development mindset is all in your head. Henry Ford said, "Whether you think you can or think you can't you're right." Commit yourself to believing you can do it and learn the techniques being offered here. Learn the basics and apply them in a thoughtful manner to help you generate positive results.

SECTION 2: NETWORKING IS THE KEY

"Always do more than is required of you."

George S. Patton, highly decorated WWII United States Army 4-Star General

There is another great quote by Jeffrey Gitomer, the self-proclaimed King of Sales, that says, "If you make a sale, you will earn a commission. If you make a friend, you will earn a fortune." There is something to be said about making friends. Friends can help us in our personal and professional lives. They have our best interests in mind and actively seek to help us. Our best friends do whatever they can to make us better versions of ourselves and help us reach our goals. You can never have too many friends.

In this section we talk about the ways you can develop new friendships focused on building a network of mutually-beneficial relationships that allow you to build a growing and sustainable practice. You will build new friendships that will allow both parties to benefit.

Sidebar: Differentiation

If you are unable to differentiate yourself, your firm, and your service from the competition, you are leaving your prospect no choice but to allow price to be the determining factor. If you are the low-cost provider, this may not be the worst thing to happen. However, there can only be one low-cost provider of legal services in a market. And if you are not that lawyer, you better learn the art of differentiation. While we'll share some initial thoughts on this subject, you should know there are other authors who have dedicated entire books to this concept, for example, *Sales Differentiation* and *Sell Different!* by Lee B. Salz. Lee is one of the most prolific experts on this topic.

Here is the first rule of differentiation: YOU![8] You are what is different from what anyone else is offering. No other firm has you working for them. You are unique and there is only one of you. And this is your most important asset in a highly competitive market. As an attorney, the clients you garner will be because you can help them solve a legal problem. Although they probably could find an attorney to represent them for less, they will choose you for your passion, expertise, empathetic approach, or whatever else you put forward as a differentiator between yourself and your competition. You are a critical part of the legal services you offer. Never forget it!

---

[8] Blount, J. (2010, Jun. 21). *People Buy You: The Real Secret to What Matters Most in Business*. Wiley.

CHAPTER 3: PROSPECTING

"Every brand isn't for everybody, and everybody isn't for every brand."

Liz Lange, American fashion designer

A prospect for a lawyer is a person who has a legal need you can fulfill. They are actively looking for a solution to a legal problem and may want to engage your services. The idea of your ideal prospect builds on this definition and includes someone whose needs nearly perfectly align with your capabilities and offerings. They recognize the value you create and would be well suited to benefit from doing business with you and your firm. In short, this would be exactly the type of person you would want to meet and speak with every day. However, you need to recognize and accept that not everyone is a good fit for you and your firm. Quite frankly, some clients are just not a good fit. In these instances, you have to discipline yourself to pass on them and focus on someone who will be a better fit.

Your ideal prospect is the person who is a good fit for doing business with your firm. Here, we will provide you with some guidance to assist you in defining the persona of your ideal prospect so you can begin your search and easily identify that person in the future.

The best place to begin is by analyzing your existing clients.

- Who are your best clients?
- What do they have in common?
- What similar characteristics and attributes define your best business relationships?
- What services do you provide for them?
- What value do you create for them?

We recommend a two-step process to help codify the types of new clients you want to attract based on your most successful current relationships. First, we will develop an ideal client company profile. Then, we will develop an ideal client contact profile. Together, these personas will allow you to best identify and pursue the types of prospects who would best align with your capabilities and offering. If you do not work directly with organizations, you can still utilize the contact persona to identify individuals most likely to be a beneficial addition to your practice.

The Pareto Principle states that 80% of your consequences (results) will come from 20% of your causes (clients). It is very possible to have challenging clients take up a disproportionate amount of your time which may cause you to neglect your absolute best clients. Perhaps it would be better to let go of these most egregious time and attention-grabbing clients so you can focus on the clientele who represent long-term and favorable relationships. While you are building your practice, be careful to keep this in mind. Not every client is the right client. It can be difficult to be picky in the beginning, but you will be better served by being selective from the start.

You can access an easy-to-use Excel worksheet at http://www.imnotinsales.com that will simplify this process. While assembling the information accurately is important, the analysis is the critical activity. You are looking to define the ideal client and prospect as the basis for your business development growth efforts.

It may actually help to take a moment to sit back, close your eyes, and envision your best client today. Who do you enjoy working with the most? Who appreciates the services you provide and the value you create? Who would you work with every day if you had the choice? The picture that comes to mind is your ideal client. We want to capture the profile of the company and the main point of contact so we can search for others of the same pedigree. You want to find additional clients who bring these same feelings to mind.

Key Characteristics and Attributes

Company Size	Revenue and Number of Employees
Industry	What do they do?
Structure	How are they organized? Sole Proprietor, Corporation, LLC?
Location	Is this a factor?
Points of Contact	Who in the organization do you need to engage? (Influencers and decision-makers)
Economic Conditions	Are they growing? Are they profitable? Are they in trouble?
Competitive Conditions	What is going on in their business? Their industry? What

	type of regulatory or economic forces are at work?
Current Firm Providing Legal Services	Who do they work with today? What can you offer to either displace or compliment those services?

Here are some examples to bring this process to life.

You specialize in work-related injury cases and worker compensation claims. You have several clients with many blue-collar employees who do manual labor outdoors. You will likely find firms in the building and highway construction industries to be among your best clients. Especially those with one hundred employees or more.

Let's suppose you assist clients with general business and tax advice. Your best clients appear to be family-owned businesses with at least $25 million in revenue who are located in your local market. These businesses focus on providing services on site to residential customers.

Now think about the people you generally interface with at these companies. Is it predominantly the owner or president of the business? What do you enjoy most about working with these individuals? What about them would you replicate in others that you work with on a regular basis? Again, we are looking for those characteristics that make you say, "Gosh, I love working with Mr. Client."

We recognize this is a new process and it may, at first glance, appear to be a fantasy. You might be thinking, "I can't pick my clients." We understand. There may be times when you are given a difficult hand. However, we have found you can often influence who is attracted to you. The type of people, and therefore companies, who end up connecting with you. You might as well work to attract ideal clients when you can. Influence what you can. It is still better than leaving it to pure chance.

CHAPTER 4: WHAT'S YOUR WHY?

"The good lawyer is the great salesman."

Janet Reno, Attorney General of the United States under the Clinton Administration

Your introductory statement is how you will create a first impression with new acquaintances and connections in a professional environment. It goes well beyond telling someone your name, title, and company. Your introductory statement tells people how you create value for others.[9] Stop and please go back and read that last sentence. Got it? Good. It is important to establish in your first interaction that you are different and your approach to connecting with people is unique, which will help make you memorable.

Humans are biased and use subconscious patterns of recognition to allow us to make quick assessments about people and situations. When we introduce ourselves, it is important to change the pattern and jolt the subconscious so it will perk up to recognize what is different. This becomes your opportunity to make a quality first impression that lasts long after the initial encounter.[10]

Never forget that it is not about you. It is about the people you can help. When you make your first

---

[9] Weinberg, M. (2012, Sept. 4). *New Sales. Simplified: The Essential Handbook for Prospecting and New Business Development*. AMACOM.

[10] Blount, J. (2017, Mar. 20). *Sales EQ: How Ultra High Performers Leverage Sales-Specific Emotional Intelligence to Close the Complex Deal.* Wiley.

impression, will you be someone they want to know and develop a relationship with? If not, they will not make the time or effort to connect with you in a meaningful way.

Remember, you never get a second chance to make a great first impression. And simply handing out business cards to everyone you meet will do little to impact your business development efforts and networking skills. You want to make an impact and anchor yourself in the mind of each potential contact.

We like to think about it in terms of TOM-TOT-WOM. That is short for Top of Mind, Tip of Tongue, and Word of Mouth. It means that you're being thought of as a resource who can help identify and solve problems, and whose contact info is worth sharing with others. From the initial meeting through your follow-up efforts, you will reinforce this causality to generate warm introductions and referrals that will propel your business development efforts to meet new clients.

Let us take a moment to consider some examples that you can use to develop your introductory statement. You can find additional examples at http://www.imnotinsales.com as well.

Example 1

Hello, my name is Fred Jones, and I am an attorney with ABC Law Firm. I work with business owners and human resource executives to help them address personnel challenges in their company and avoid potentially expensive litigation.

Example 2

Hello, my name is Fred Jones, and I am an attorney with ABC Law Firm. I work with financial professionals to help them, and their clients, develop wills and trusts to protect their family's assets and ensure their final wishes are honored.

Example 3

Hi there. I couldn't help but overhear your situation. You look like you'd appreciate having a divorce attorney you can trust and who won't break the bank. My name is Fred Jones from ABC Law Firm. I specialize in helping fathers like you navigate the complexity of divorce while protecting your parental rights and financial wellbeing.

Now, take a moment to draft your own introductory statement. Remember, give thought to how you help others and the value you create for your clients. We recommend that once you complete this task you engage a trusted friend to rehearse. Tell them what you are looking to accomplish and ask them to evaluate your introduction. You can fine-tune the wording and delivery accordingly. You want this to be a genuine statement of how you help other people because that is what people you meet will find most compelling and memorable.

Follow-Up Questions

Once you introduce yourself, the next thing to do is draw the person into a conversation. You do this simply by asking their name, where they work, and what brings them to this event or meeting. Are they a member? If so, how long have they been involved with this group? What do they find most beneficial about participating? You want to get the other person talking and sharing. People love to talk about themselves. Give the person the opportunity to share their thoughts and feelings with you to build a connection that will lead to a relationship. After all, it's a conversation, not an interrogation.

And this is important: when someone is sharing details of their life with you, be sure to be in the moment. To be actively listening by acknowledging what they are saying with an occasional nod, a smile, or a brief comment that compliments, but does not interrupt them. For example, "that's interesting" or "good to know" or "tell me more" are phrases that demonstrate you are engaged, interested, and desire to learn more about them and their situation. If during the discussion there is a topic that really resonates with you, ask if you could set another time to discuss it in more detail. Then you are securing another meeting but keeping your focus on the topic.

Remember too, the more the other person engages you in the discussion, the more you will learn about them, and the more interesting you will be. Yes, you will be more interesting without saying a word. It is one of the nuances of human conversation. The reason we find people who are good listeners interesting is because we enjoy talking about ourselves. As a result, the more we get to talk about ourselves the more we tend to like the person we are speaking to. Odd but true.

Learning to become a great listener is the first step in becoming a great conversationalist and increasing your likability. People want to become friends and do business with people they like. To be likable requires that you be genuine and authentic. People can read through insincerity. Simply have a genuine interest in learning about the person you're speaking to without any ulterior motives. If there is a business opportunity to be discussed, let it unfold organically. Don't force the issue. Be engaging and be likable.

Here are some initial questions you can use to help start a conversation. Having a few "go-to" questions prepared will make it easier for you to focus on the conversation and actively listen to what the other person is saying. Unfortunately, when most people have a conversation, they spend too much time thinking about what they want to say next rather than truly listening and understanding. Focus on actively listening to the responses before asking your next question. Pause between questions. Take a breath. Count to two. And don't interrupt in your eagerness to ask your next question either. It will help to differentiate you and improve your likeability.

- Is this your first time at this event?
- What made you want to attend?
- What do you think about the event so far?
- Are you local to the area?
- How long have you been a (occupation)?
- How did you decide to become a (occupation)?
- When did you first join this association or group?

- What do you find most beneficial about being a member?
- Are you involved with any of the committees?
- What advice would you give to someone new like me?
- Who are the key influencers in this group? Could you introduce me to them?

You can certainly build upon this list to have other questions prepared. Being prepared will increase your confidence and allow you to be more productive at networking events. It is not much different than attending a dinner party where you do not know all the guests. You want to meet some new people and just need to prime the conversation pump to get things going.

We recognize that some of you may not initially enjoy networking events and "small talk." We will not waste your time convincing you to feel differently. What we can tell you with certainty is a critical component of the business development process. While you may not always find it enjoyable meeting new people, you might find that developing new relationships, where some may develop into genuine friendships, is rewarding.

It is important to acknowledge the role you will play in building mutually beneficial relationships. People need to "buy" you first. You are an essential part of the difference being offered in a competitive marketplace.

Networking Groups

We would also recommend you join online groups where your clients and prospects are members or that align with your profession and interests, or both. If you search for groups, you will discover there are thousands to choose from and the list continues to grow. These groups also have a significant following which will dramatically increase your exposure.

Some groups allow anyone to join. Others require that you "apply" which means that someone will review your profile when you click the "join" button to ensure you are a good fit for the group. Then, once you are a member, you will be able to post material in the group.

This means that whatever you post will have the opportunity to be seen by a much larger audience.

Here are a few potential groups:

- Law.com (over 10,000 members)
- e-LEGAL (over 250,000 members)
- Inhouse Legal (over 100,000 members)
- GST, Tax & Legal Compliance (over 50,000 members)
- Family Law Professionals (over 20,000 members)

There are some groups that allow anyone to post material at any time. Other groups require content to be reviewed prior to being visible to the group. In this case, you create a post like normal but may not see it for a few days (or more) while it is being reviewed, approved, and posted. You should keep this in mind when posting time sensitive information.

You can also start making individual connections with members in the group as you get to know them. When you post an item in your main feed, your connections are the most likely see your post. Your circle of influence grows when they see your content on your main page and either like or comment on the post. It now funnels into their feed so their connections can also see it. From there, it can expand further as others like or comment on the post.

You can also post non-legal related items as well. If you have a passion for history, you could occasionally post information about an upcoming reenactment. The act of positing and sharing various types of information contributes to the overall goal of becoming more familiar to your groups and connections and increasing your exposure. Someone in another group unrelated to your business might see your post, click on your profile, and decide to engage you on a legal matter because they have been impressed by your deep knowledge and interest in some other topic.

Networking groups are a great way to increase your influence and to have your content seen by those in your target audience. We will go into more detail on professional social media networks in a later chapter.

Networking Tip

Vince here. To be candid, I did not always find it easy to attend a networking event where I did not know anyone. As an introvert, it was stressful and difficult to attend these functions even though I knew it was essential to find new business. However, I developed this strategy, which helped me immensely. Instead of walking around hoping someone would approach me, I would survey the room for anyone standing alone. I then discovered that by walking over and introducing myself to this fellow "loner," that they were happy to have someone to talk to. What's more, the connection always evolved into an introduction and a pleasant conversation.

But that's not all. I next would look around to see if anyone else was standing alone and I'd invite that person to join us in our conversation. Next thing you know, there are four or five of us in the group sharing stories just like everyone else in the hall. Each of these people were thankful that I included them in the group, for making introductions, and for helping forge a few new relationships that would ensure they would look forward to attending the next event.

While business associates and connections are initially desired, your ability to build friendships will be the most rewarding part. In the end, it is your friends who take the greatest interest in your wellbeing and success. Your friends will be the ones to go the extra mile to help you when you need it. Your friends will be the ones who will keep you top of mind and look for opportunities to recommend your services and refer business to you. Yes, you need more friends. Friends are the key to a happy and successful life.

CHAPTER 5: CONSISTENT CONSISTENCY

"It's not all about talent. It's about dependability, consistency, and being able to improve. If you work hard and you're coachable, and you understand what you need to do, you can improve."

Bill Belichick, Six-time Super Bowl winning coach of the NFL's New England Patriots

There is literally an endless array of material dedicated to the art of follow up and nearly every professional development book discusses it at length. Yet, one of the biggest challenges to achieving a business development mindset is to be consistent in communication with your clients. You might ask why this is important? Well, part of the reason is that we need to better value relationships. Relationships take time and energy to cultivate. And given today's society of instant gratification, many people, including lawyers, are unwilling to invest the time that it takes to engage in relationship building and consistently following up with their prospective clients.

Remember, you have competition. You may not always think about it, but there are other attorneys and firms that can deliver the same services as you. We respect the fact that you and your firm may be better in many ways. But not everyone who is looking to establish a relationship with an attorney will know that. It is incumbent upon you to earn the relationship and convey the true value you and your firm can create for your clients.

To help you see the benefit of regular contact with your prospects, here are some compelling statistics that will help us illustrate the point.

- 80% of sales engagements require five follow-up calls after the first meeting. As a lawyer, are you investing this amount of time in cultivating prospective clients?
- Or are you like 44% of professionals who give up after just one follow-up?
- After four follow-ups, 94% of professionals have given up.

Let's reiterate; **80% of developing relationships that generate business require five follow ups but 94% of business development professionals give up after just four attempts**. This means that if you are just willing to be a bit more tenacious and keep reaching out to your prospects, you will be in the **top six percent** of business development professionals willing to take the time to build meaningful client relationships. If you're not willing to do what it takes, then you are simply wasting your time. This information is powerful and can further help to differentiate you from your competition by showing your prospect that they matter to you and that they are worth your time.

A best practice for engaging with a prospect or client is to have a call to action with every interaction. It does not matter whether it is an email, phone call, a video call, or in-person meeting, it is YOUR responsibility to identify the next step to keep the conversation moving forward. A typical call to action is to schedule your next meeting. But a call to action might also include a request for documents or an introduction to a stakeholder regarding a potential case. Regardless, failure to do this may find you spending countless hours calling, emailing, and sending carrier pigeons to re-engage your prospect or client.

Learn from the Past

Learning is a continuous process. Some of our most important lessons come from our mistakes. If we look at our failures as opportunities for self improvement and for bettering our approach in the future, then we are demonstrating a business development mindset. Here are some proven strategies that can help you:

- View feedback as a gift,

- If you lose a client, take the time to ask where you came up short,

- Remain objective and see every situation of disappointment as an opportunity for growth, and

- We cannot control what goes on outside our office, but we can (and must!) control what goes on inside of it.

Be Positive…Always

Negativity becomes a self-fulfilling prophecy. Reframe the way you view failure to focus on the positive.

- If you're wondering why you're struggling to attract and retain clients, the first thing you should check is your attitude.

- Baseball is a numbers game; failure is built into the system. If you fail seven out of ten times in baseball, you're going to the Hall of Fame.

- Do not embrace failure. Be resolute and strive for success.

Competitive Advantage

Be familiar with what competing law firms offer so you can readily differentiate yourself from their approach.

Be able to answer:

1. Why should your prospect make a change in their current legal representation?
2. What is it about you or your firm that should cause your prospect to choose you to represent them?
3. Why should your prospect act now?

Communicate More Effectively

Before you can get prospective clients to "like" you, you must first learn to communicate with them in a purposeful way. Understanding a bit of brain science would be helpful here. When determining meaning, the mind processes communication in accordance with the following engagement:

- 7% verbal

- 38% vocal tone
- 55% visual[11]

Which means that 93% of communication is "nonverbal." To be effective, you need to have a communication style that is not purely dependent on verbal engagement. Knowing how to correspond persuasively in writing is incredibly important. Not to worry, we will cover these skills later in this workbook.

Build Trust

Trust-building is more than a social process; it's also a neurological one that stimulates brain endorphins for connecting emotions. To build trust, a lawyer needs to increase a prospect's levels of oxytocin (trust), dopamine (happiness), and serotonin (relaxation) by…

---

[11] The University of Texas Permian Basin. (n.d.). *How Much of Communication is Nonverbal?* The University of Texas Permian Basin. Retrieved November 16, 2022 from https://online.utpb.edu/about-us/articles/communication/how-much-of-communication-is-nonverbal/#:~:text=It%20was%20Albert%20Mehrabian%2C%20a,%2C%20and%207%25%20words%20only.

- Establishing Credibility: Provide helpful advice and information so your customer will begin to count on you and see your legal acumen and attention to their legal situation.

- Demonstrate Empathy: Take a personable approach and remember you're talking to another person. Don't speak like a robot. Step into their shoes, be truthful and honest, build connections, allow your prospective client to talk and explain themselves, and listen.

- Use Nonverbal Cues: Your tone of voice matters twice as much as the message itself. The best way to moderate your tone of voice is to use pitch variation and avoid sounding monotone, slow down when speaking, and use expressive speech.

- Be Consistent: Be predictable. When you say you're going to do something, do it. A prospective client is much more likely to trust you if your behavior is consistent over time, which reduces their fear and increases their level of oxytocin. The best way to do this is to follow a defined engagement process.

- Make a Connection: Social reinforcement states that people want to be around people who possess opinions and worldviews that validate their own. This can be as simple as finding a mutual connection on LinkedIn. Once a connection is made, oxytocin levels increase, which can lead to a more meaningful connection.[12]

[12] Zak, P.J. (2017). *The Neuroscience of Trust: Management behaviors that foster employee engagement.* Harvard Business Review. Retrieved November 16, 2022, from https://hbr.org/2017/01/the-neuroscience-of-trust

SECTION 3: GREAT MINDS THINK ALIKE

"Success occurs when opportunity meets preparation."

Zig Ziglar, American author, salesman, and motivational speaker for personal development

When undertaking a new venture, it is important to surround yourself with positivity and to not be distracted by naysayers. In this regard, developing a network of like-minded professionals is critically important.

Building a strong and supportive network requires a cognitive effort of thoughtful engagement. You have to think about who you can engage with and who will empower and encourage you in your journey to acquire a business development mindset to help you grow your legal practice.

You will find that once you surround yourself with a circle of positivity, you will be better able to circumvent and overcome the obstacles of self-doubt and feelings of inadequacy that are natural whenever you attempt something new.

Sidebar: The Importance of Likeability

As lawyers, you will find that clients are more likely to hire you if they like you. It is important to realize that regardless of your legal expertise, clients work with lawyers they can relate to and who can relate to them. Hiring a lawyer is a significant expense. When it comes to making the decision to hire a lawyer, you will find the client's perception of you is critically important. Now, I know what you might be thinking, I'm likable! Of course, you are. We all believe that we are likable, and for the most part, this is true. However, there are ways in which you can increase your likeability and improve your ability to develop a mutually-beneficial relationship. Here are some questions that every prospective client considers when they are assessing whether or not to have you and your firm represent them:[13]

1. Do I like you?
2. Do you listen to me?
3. Do you make me feel important?
4. Do you understand me and my problems?
5. Do I trust and believe you?
6. Do we share the same values?
7. Do I feel that you have my best interest in mind?
8. Would I recommend you to a friend or colleague?
9. Are you reliable and consistent?
10. Would I do business with you if the roles were reversed?

---

[13] Blount, J. (2017, Mar. 20). *Sales EQ: How Ultra High Performers Leverage Sales-Specific Emotional Intelligence to Close the Complex Deal*. Wiley. p. 163.

You should think about these questions in every engagement and make sure you can honestly answer, on the prospective client's behalf, 'yes' to each. Remember, how you interact with your client will drive their response to each question. Each little thing you do, or don't do, will contribute to generating either 'yes' or 'no' answer for each question. Again, people are emotional more than they are rational. You must motivate them to have a positive emotional response to you, and this is accomplished by what you say, how you say it, and what you do (your behavior during each interaction). You are either pulling them closer or pushing them away. Be sure to pull them closer.

CHAPTER 6: LAW OF ATTRACTION

"Networking is an investment in your business. It takes time and when done correctly can yield great results for years to come."

Diane Helbig, American author, speaker, and small business sales coach

Referrals are the most powerful and important introductions you can receive. When you receive a referral from someone it says, "I trust this person and so should you." Building a business that can grow and prosper from referrals is the holy grail of every legal professional. As Alan Weiss said, "referrals are the coinage of my realm."[14] We absolutely agree. The question is, where to begin?

You need to start by understanding that referrals are based on trust. When someone trusts you enough to tell a friend, family member, or business associate to contact you, they are providing you with their highest compliment. In many cases, the people being referred will not shop around or compare alternatives. They are coming to you because of the trust they have in the person that made the recommendation. The circle of trust is interlinked. It is essential to understand this dynamic since it will be the cornerstone to generating and receiving future referrals.

---

[14] Weiss, A. (2021, Jun. 22). *The Consulting Bible: How to Launch and Grow a Seven-Figure Consulting Business*. Wiley.

Different Types of Lead Generators

There are distinct types of lead generators, and you will need to become competent in cultivating each type.

The first type of lead generator is a business referral. In this case, someone you know refers a prospect who has a stated need for the services you provide. This is the best type of referral since the person has a need that you can address. You may receive this referral from a current client, a colleague, or friend experienced with your work. Remember, this referral is a high compliment since the person is specifically recommending you because of the trust they have in you. While it is great to receive referrals there is nothing that prevents you from actively soliciting them as well. This is where lawyers with a business development mindset excel. They recognize that the larger their circle of connection, the better the opportunity to develop new relationships that can lead to future business. In business you can never know or be connected to too many people. The objective is to understand the types of potential connections and build a network that incorporates each type to build a pipeline of future opportunities.

The second type of lead generator is a suspect. In this case the person may not have a specific or immediate need but may require your services in the future. If you work with accountants, for example, you might receive an introduction from someone who knows an accountant. While there may be no immediate need at this time, you know from experience that they may eventually need your services.

More importantly, if you generally work with accountants, the more accountants you know the better. Who better to make additional introductions to your target audience than someone inside your target audience?

A third type of lead generator is a connector. Here the person will most likely not need your services directly but is someone who knows others who may be a good prospect for you. A connector is a person who is proficient at making strategic introductions. You can consider them a business matchmaker. Having access to connectors is important since they enjoy making strategic introductions and often have a wide circle of acquaintances.

Proactive Referral Generation

We all appreciate a great referral. However, even under the best circumstances, you will not receive enough referrals without being proactive. In this section we will review the separate ways to generate additional referrals by simply asking for them.

Your current clients remain one of the best sources for the three major types of lead generators. They are familiar with you and the work you perform and are connected to others in your target audience. If you have any reservations about asking for referrals dismiss those negative thoughts. Remember, the person you are about to ask for a referral is working with you. Which means, unless there are extenuating circumstances, they like you and will welcome the opportunity to help you. All you need to do is ask them.

Example 1: Request A Referral

In this example you are requesting a referral for someone who has needs that are similar to those of your client.

You are looking for them to connect you with someone who may need your services in the near future.

You: I am happy to hear you are pleased with the services we have provided you. May I ask you a favor?

Client: Certainly!

You: Would you happen to know anyone else who might benefit from working with me?

Client: Actually, I do. You should speak with Susan Jenkins at ABC Company.

You: Excellent. Would you be willing to introduce us?

Client: Absolutely. I will call her tomorrow and arrange for us to have coffee together.

You: Thank you. I appreciate your willingness to help me very much.

Example 2: Request a Warm Introduction

In this example you are looking for potential prospects. These are people in the same line of business as your client and who may need your services at some point in the future.

You: I am happy to hear that you are pleased with the services we have provided you. May I ask you a favor?

Client: Absolutely.

You: Would you have any recommendations for other people, like yourself, (accountants, financial planners, etc.) who I should meet?

Client: Actually, I can think of two or three people who would benefit from knowing you.

You: That is great. Would you be willing to make an introduction?

Client: Yes, I would be happy to do so.

You: Thank you. I appreciate your willingness to help me very much.

Example 3: Leveraging LinkedIn Connections

Often you can ask someone who is willing to provide a referral and they just get stumped. No one immediately comes to mind, and it creates that awkward situation where you both end up staring at each other in silence until you finally say, "don't worry about it." A perfectly good opportunity lost to a case of stage fright.

You can reduce the odds of a negative response by accepting responsibility for doing the work for your client. If you are connected to them on LinkedIn (and you should be), take a moment to go through their list of connections to identify any good potential contacts. Instead of counting on them to think of a name on the spot, come to the discussion with three or four names you found in their LinkedIn network and ask them for an introduction. This is a fantastic way to focus on your target audience and receive assistance that is meaningful.

You: I noticed that you are connected to Joe Roberts on LinkedIn. How well do you know Joe?

Client: Very well. We have done business together on several occasions.

You: I would appreciate an introduction to Joe. I think I could be a resource to him and his company. Would you be willing to introduce us over coffee or lunch? Or perhaps call him on my behalf?

Client: I would be happy to arrange a lunch meeting. I have been meaning to call Joe anyway.

Taking the time to research potential connections alleviates the stress for your client and positions you to earn a referral proactively. We think that if you took a few minutes each week to review the people your connections know that you could easily develop a list of potential introductions that could lead to new relationships and potentially new business. This is one of the calendar activities you should schedule with yourself to ensure it gets accomplished.

And don't discount the power provided by a letter of recommendation. In this instance, you're asking for an open referral in the form of a testimonial. The letter of recommendation is something you can share with prospective clients to help demonstrate your expertise. It is also a great way to show a prospect that you were able to help a client who is like them with the same type of need. By demonstrating the alignment between your referral and your prospect, you are leveraging something called tribal social proof. This is a great way to help your prospect feel at ease that your services can be of benefit to them.

The only thing preventing you from receiving more referrals is asking for them. Now, get to work!

CHAPTER 7: BIRDS OF A FEATHER

"A man only learns in two ways, one by reading, and the other by association with smarter people."

Will Rogers, American cowboy, writer, and humorist

Today there are many diverse types of associations for every profession. We are confident that you are familiar with some of the key associations for the legal profession, such as the American Bar Association or the National Association for Legal Professionals. These associations exist to promote the best interests of their members and to facilitate the advancement of your profession.

Becoming a member of your specific association will provide you a host of benefits including access to other professionals doing the same or similar work, industry learning events, information about trends and developments, and the opportunity to network with other professionals and vendors servicing the industry. It is a wonderful way to stay connected to your profession and to stay current with trends and developments. We highly recommend it.

You may also consider joining an association that represents your ideal client profile. Consider which organizations your current clients and peers participate in? Birds of a feather flock together. You may want to ask your key clients about their professional activities and see if there is an opportunity to participate as an associate or member. You can also see what groups they belong to on LinkedIn and join those as well. Often there are sponsorship opportunities which can provide you greater visibility to your target persona by demonstrating your commitment to being a sustaining member of their group.

Sponsorship programs and levels vary so you should investigate what makes the most sense for you and your firm. Among the most common benefits beyond attending meetings and functions is being able to access an event attendee list, submit articles for their newsletter, join a committee, make a presentation to the group, and have your firm's logo prominently displayed at events or in related publications. This is certainly in line with other marketing efforts, except that it is highly directed towards your ideal client profile. This will provide you many opportunities to meet similar minded professionals and build your network in your target market. Make sure you are regularly in touch with five to ten people in your industry. One way to accomplish this is to join a committee, board, or group. If you make a good impression, these contacts could lead to deeper relationships and referrals.

Tip 1: Look Before You Leap!

Every group will have their own policies governing membership types and the related fees. Before joining a group, contact the leader and ask if they allow guests to attend a meeting or two to meet the participants and see if there is a fit. Most groups are happy to accommodate this request and it will give you the opportunity to see if the group is worthy of your time. Do not fall into the trap of purchasing membership to organizations you will not attend on a regular basis. Further, membership is a good start, but to maximize your investment consider your level of participation. Consider joining a committee or volunteering to assist in other ways. This will allow you to meet more people and demonstrate your commitment to being a productive member of the organization.

Occasionally a group only offers membership to those who are "invited" by a current member. Do not let that discourage you. Contact the group leader and make an inquiry. Invite them to coffee to learn more about the group and the benefits of association. You may find that person is willing to sponsor your application, or there is someone else you know who is currently a member. Most organizations are very motivated to expand their membership and will be willing to help the right candidates find a way to join.

Tip 2: Build Relationships First

Some groups, like Business Networking International (BNI), will require you to bring leads or referrals for other participants each meeting. In general, be sure you get to know the other members before you offer a referral. Remember, when you tell one of your clients to speak with another service provider, they are trusting that you know that person and their capabilities. Your reputation is on the line. Take the time to build a relationship with new associates by inviting them to coffee or lunch outside the normal meeting schedule. Learn about their business, clients, and family. Share details about you as well to develop a true friendship that will lead to a mutually beneficial business relationship.

An easy strategy is to schedule "meet & greets" on your calendar. Simply call people you meet at events and ask them to join you for coffee or lunch. Be sure to use the right vernacular when approaching someone. What would be more appealing to you, "Hello Tom, I would like to schedule some time on your calendar to meet" or "Hello Tom, I was hoping we could get together for a visit to chat"? Would you rather attend a meeting or schedule a visit to chat? While there is certainly a time and place for formality it is not preferred when you are trying to establish friendships. And while you can certainly invite someone to the ubiquitous coffee, some folks might not drink coffee. So, be whimsical and offer them the option of meeting you for ice cream too. Yes, the goal is to build a network of friends, not just business acquaintances. Friends will be much more interested in helping you succeed. Plus, you can never have too many friends in life.

Tip 3: You Have to Give to Get

Once you have started to develop a good working relationship for some of the group's members, take the initiative to offer them a referral or introduction. It can be as simple as, "George, I have a client who may need the services you offer. I would like to make an introduction. Is that good with you?" Of course! We all love a referral! You will certainly get a positive response and begin the process of making mutual introductions.

Giving a referral away will activate the law of reciprocity. It is a psychological term that states when someone receives a "gift" from you they will feel obliged to return the favor. They will actively look for ways to return kindness with kindness. As you offer introductions ("gifts") to others, they will be looking for ways to return the favor by making introductions for you. It is a powerful way to start the process of sharing connections and generating new conversations.

Tip 4: Active Participation Required

Simply joining a group or two will not be sufficient to generate business. There are lots of stories of people spending significant sums to join a group with no results. It takes a concerted effort to build relationships that lead to introductions and referral business. You must be committed to developing a plan and then working that plan to generate the best results.

Some of these groups have committees that help organize events. Joining a committee is a fantastic way to show you are committed and to accelerate your integration with the group. You will get the chance to meet more people who can help you get connected to the other members. This will certainly accelerate your ability to make the connections necessary to develop the right relationships.

While some organizations may not allow associate members to join a committee all need help setting up for meetings or other events. A great way to meet people is to offer to help at the sign in table where name badges are distributed. Think about it. They will be lining up to see you! There is no better way to meet a lot of new people, and gain immediate exposure, than by helping them locate their name badge and welcoming them to the event. It will also make it easier to approach people and strike up a conversation later since they will remember meeting you when they first arrived. No experience required. Just courage.

You should conduct your own search to find those that best meet your profession as well as who are geographically desirable. Some of the national organizations have local chapters you can join. Your local Chamber of Commerce is often a suitable place to start. Be sure to consult with them about specific subgroups that meet which may offer you access to a more targeted audience best suited for your business.

Tip 5: Connect with the Leadership Team

When you attend your first networking or association event make a point of introducing yourself to the leadership team. You can identify the key players in advance by reviewing their website or by asking when you arrive and sign in. It is a terrific way to connect with those people who clearly have a personal stake in the success of the group. These people also are motivated to attract new members. They may be helpful in making some initial introductions to other influential members to help you feel comfortable and to encourage you to participate further. This is a wonderful way to evaluate the quality of the group and to determine if you want to pursue membership.

Tip 6: Leverage Your Vendors

You and your firm have a host of vendors that supply a variety of products and services you need to operate your law practice. When was the last time you asked them for a referral or introduction?

Once you take the time to clearly understand your ideally qualified prospect, asking for a referral will become much easier. Let us suppose you represent construction companies against insurance claims who do about $25 to $35 million in annual revenue. Instead of asking a vendor, let us say the company that provides your firm with their copiers and printers, "is there anyone you can introduce me to?" you should ask the sales professional "Do you have clients in the construction industry doing about $25 million a year in business?"

While they may not be able to generate a list of ten companies, they might very well know one or two. You may ask them to inquire amongst their peers for any similar companies their organization has a client. This may increase the list to five or six. In short order you have just identified some potential prospects. Imagine if you could receive just five introductions from each of your top ten vendors; that would be fifty potential new opportunities. No, not everyone will develop into a client. However, if two or three did become a client, what would that mean for you, your practice group, and your firm overall?

Take advantage of their willingness to meet to ensure your happiness and to provide an inside view of many other local businesses. You will be amazed at the level of insight the sales professional for that company can provide and their willingness to assist you. They are constantly working to create value for you. They have competition as well and know that their ability to create value will set them apart from their competitors and create more loyalty. Give them the chance to help you in ways beyond just the product or service you purchase from them. We guarantee they will be more than willing to help. All you need to do is ask.

Suggested Professional Organizations

In Appendix A, we are providing an overview of some of the professional organizations and associations you may want to consider. This list is far from all-inclusive, and we recommend that you investigate what is available in your local community and in your area of specialization. Ask colleagues and friends which organizations they belong to develop new opportunities. Perhaps they would be willing to bring you to the next event so you could see if there is value in participating. In addition to local events many organizations host regional and national meetings that may be worth attending. Look for notices in your local business journal or search the web for upcoming events and activities. You may likely find several opportunities available to attend.

Where Are Your Clients?

In addition to joining an association for your own professional development, you may also want to consider attending events your top clients, and potential new clients, attend. If you do work with business owners in the construction industry, ask them with which groups or associations they hold membership. Perhaps they would be willing to have you attend an event with them to learn more. Remember this analogy: when you go duck hunting, the most important thing to remember is to go where the ducks are. And, as you probably already know, birds of a feather tend to flock together. Attending these events is a fantastic opportunity to meet new potential clients and expand your network.

There are certainly many opportunities to network and grow your professional connections. Quite frankly, it can be difficult to attend all the events you could or should attend given other priorities. We suggest that you consider developing a team from your firm who are also interested in attending similar events and work together to cover the various events without any one person having to do all the work. For the larger events, you may want to attend as a group and work independently to cover the smaller venues.

CHAPTER 8: EXPANDING YOUR REACH

"Your network is your net worth."

Porter Gale, American marketing and branding expert

This section will discuss how to extend your sales mindset to your online brand and persona, and the importance of portraying a professional image. The right portrayal can be a gateway to developing new connections and business. The wrong message can scare people away.

If you have not recently performed an Internet search of your name this would be a suitable place to start. What immediately pops up? What information is available about you, accurate or otherwise, that someone might find conducting a search of their own? Do you have a common name that brings forth information about another person that might be confused with you? You may be surprised by what you find. As you already know, your reputation is the culmination of all aspects of your life. Be sure to guard it carefully.

We recommend periodic searches of your name in various search engines, to evaluate your online presence and to ensure the information is accurate. Remember, the Internet does not offer an eraser; once something is posted it can be a challenge to get it permanently removed. Be careful what you post and share or what others, even family and friends, post about you.

Also be careful what your friends share that is connected to you. While this may be harder to control, it is still important to ensure you have a squeaky-clean online presence. Ask yourself this question, "Would this be something I would want my mother to know about?" If the answer is "no," it would probably be a good idea not to share it with the world.

Professional Social Media Networks

Professional social media networks, such as LinkedIn, are great tools to promote your professional image and brand. It is a conduit to connecting with other professionals and provides a communication platform for you to demonstrate thought leadership. This is a way for you to reach out to potential connections as well as potential connections and clients locating you. Having a professional looking profile page is essential to creating your online persona as a competent and trustworthy attorney.

The first thing you will need to do is to conduct an honest assessment of your current profile. If you do not have one, you will want to create one using this guide. You may want to consider viewing the profiles of well-known attorneys in your field or attorneys at other local firms. This will give you an idea of what they are or are not doing. It will also show you if they are involved in any civic or professional organizations that you may want to consider joining. This reconnaissance is something you might want to consider doing a few times per year to keep tabs on other professionals in your specialty.

The following is intended to be a checklist to ensure that your online presence accurately and positively portrays your professionalism. There is also a great deal of information available from other sources and service providers who can help you further.

Profile Photo

- A professional profile on LinkedIn starts with a professional headshot. It is worth the small investment to have a professional photographer take some pictures with different backgrounds, or if you feel confident taking your own pictures, today's cell phone cameras can also get the job done. The whole idea here is to present the best image of yourself.

Background Photo or (Banner Image)

- This should be something that catches the eye and perhaps represents your offering. It may be as simple as your firm's logo, a picture of a courtroom, or you in a conference room giving a presentation.

Name

- Your formal name as well as your preferred name. For example, your name may be "Richard", but you prefer to be called "Rich." You can modify it to read: Richard "Rich" Surname.

Headline (Statement of Differentiation)

- Your headline is visible in your likes, comments, and activity; make it count. Ensure it's specific enough to indicate how you are different from others with the role or title. You should also view your headline much as a shopkeeper looks at his display window. The display window gets changed so that it keeps the attention of the passersby. Your headline statement should also be refreshed on a regular basis so that it does not become stale.

Current Position

Education – Show in Introduction

Industry

About Statement

- This is a good opportunity to revisit your introductory statement and speak to who you typically work with and help. This is not only the place to tell your "me" story, but also your "why" story.

Featured

- This will show content you have previously posted. It is a nice archive of information that new connections may want to review to learn more about you as a subject matter expert.

Experience

- You want to keep it relevant, so list only the most recent positions held. To reiterate, LinkedIn is not the place to post your resume. Rather, you are creating a narrative and only posting the work experience that is relevant to the story you want to tell.

Education

- Degrees conferred and majors, if applicable. Also, if you are junior and feel that your age may be held against you for being inexperienced, do not feel compelled to post the years in which you attended university or law school.

Licenses and Certifications

- When you are entering this information, you may find the "branded" version (logo) has already been uploaded and is available for use.

Volunteer Experience

- Do you coach a team? Volunteer at your child's school? Provide pro bono services? This is an area where people can see the human side of you. It is also a place where you can connect with prospective clients who share similar interests.

Skills and Endorsements

- You may want to focus on items most closely related to the work you currently do. There is a limitation for the number of skills you can claim or be recommended. You can also add skills through LinkedIn Learning by watching videos on a wide range of topics. This may be a way to broaden your perspective.

Recommendations

- This is a great place to solicit recommendations from peers and clients. It will show how many recommendations you have given as well as received. If you have not focused on this area in the past, you may want to start by writing a few recommendations for other people who you respect and admire as a way of encouraging others to reciprocate. You can also consider requesting a recommendation from someone you know like a professor, a previous supervisor, or the leader of a non-profit or organization where you volunteered. It does not have to speak to your work as an attorney. These are testimonials about you as a person as much as they are about you as a professional.

Accomplishments

- Awards from work, the legal profession, or from your efforts as a volunteer. Again, this information provides some insights into who you are and what others recognize about you. Don't be bashful.

Interests

- An area to disclose items about your personal life including hobbies or activities you enjoy.

Publications

- Add your articles, blog posts, and speaking engagements to showcase evidence of thought leadership and recognized expertise. This is a great way to demonstrate how others respect your opinions and guidance. It is more powerful when others recognize your credentials than when you try to promote your expertise directly.

One of the best tools offered on social media sites like LinkedIn is the ability to post original content or share links to other content that might be of interest to your connections. Whether you are creating or curating content, posting is a fantastic way to become recognized for your passion and expertise. This can improve your professional reputation and online presence.

There are some easy tools to determine the success of your efforts on LinkedIn. We recommend that you make visiting your LinkedIn profile a daily activity. It should be an appointment on your calendar for the same time each day. You can check on what is being posted, review updates from colleagues, make comments, and check for connection invitations.

There is also a great way to measure your progress using the LinkedIn Social Selling Index (SSI). It is free to access, and you can do so by going to https://www.linkedin.com/sales/ssi?src=liother&veh=www.linkedin.com. Your SSI score will have several components listed below.

1. Industry SSI Rank: how you compare to others in your industry
2. Network SSI Rank: how you compare to others in your network
3. Current Social Selling Index: an overall score for you with 100 being the best possible score. This is composed of four critical areas: Your professional brand; Connecting with the right people; Engaging with insights; and Building relationships.

LinkedIn Social Selling Index (SSI)

This is not a tool you want to check daily. However, it would be a good idea to establish a baseline before you initiate any changes to your profile or how you use LinkedIn today. This way you can have a starting point to measure and evaluate your progress. Thereafter we recommend checking it once a month and recording the score so you can track the change. Improvement, and trending over time.

Your connections will consist of all the people you know either personally or virtually. You will have to make your own decisions about accepting invitations from people you do not know personally. A good tip is to see what connections you have in common, which is displayed in the invitation. This can be an effective way of expanding your network while maintaining a sense of security. As you improve your reach by being active with posting material, and responding to posts with your own comments, you may find people being attracted to you and wanting to connect. Some of these people may be future clients or connectors.

Seeing who has viewed your profile is one of our favorite features. Take a moment to review this list for potential networking opportunities. There are many reasons someone may have viewed your profile. Perhaps they were searching for someone with your skill set, or for alumni, or association members. If you see that someone has viewed your profile and you are not currently connected, you may want to consider sending them an invitation to connect.

LinkedIn provides you the opportunity to share content which others in your network, and beyond, can view. This is an excellent opportunity to elevate your position as a thought leader and influencer. Posting content on a regular basis will increase your visibility as well as increase the probability you will appear in a search on a specific topic or skill set. Repetition builds reputation. It is a wonderful way to increase your exposure and expand your virtual presence.

Remember, you are working to remain top of mind to anyone who might need your services or is able to refer or introduce you to someone who needs your services. You can best accomplish this by giving; give away information to create value for others. It is quick, easy, and demonstrates your commitment to help others. In return, they will want to help you.

Create or curate? Both options work well in combination. You may have read an interesting article or seen a unique post recently. The topic is associated with your area of expertise or the law or business in general. It is something that would be of interest to people with whom you often associate. This is a perfect opportunity to curate a post to share this information. When posting, be sure to include an explanatory paragraph addressing why this article was interesting to you so you can make an authentic connection with your network. Contribute to your network by sharing credible information pertinent to them and their business.

Example 1:

I was researching the new IRS tax code for a client and discovered there are some notable exceptions to the new rule that could have a positive effect when filing your tax returns. This information will help us provide better guidance to our clients and ensure they are properly positioned for their next tax filing. The article with all the details can be found here: samplearticle.com.

You may also want to consider creating your own content to post and share. Perhaps you recently finished reading a book, or attended a conference, or discovered some interesting information while researching an issue. Consider authoring a post on what you learned and why it might be important to your ideal client or other attorneys in your practice area. LinkedIn gives you two options for posting your original content. You can choose the long form option of authoring an article, or the short form option of sharing a post within a 3,000-character limit. You may want to include your own impressions and the significance to your client or practice (without disclosing anything considered confidential).

Example 2:

I was fortunate to attend a presentation by Robert Smith of Smith Investigative Services at the (Insert Town Name) Rotary Club this week. Fascinating information about how to retain and engage a professional investigator when you need to gather evidence for a case or other pending legal matter. Mr. Smith is a well-known speaker and author with nearly 30 years of practical experience in law enforcement and as an independent investigator. The link to his website is: smithinvestigations.com.

As you can see, the posts you create do not have to be long or overly detailed. You are simply sharing some news or information to pique the interest of others. If it does not apply to them, they will skip over it. If it catches their attention, they can access the additional details. Either way, they will associate the sharing of expertise with you which will help you develop a reputation as a subject matter expert who is willing to share information.

SECTION 4: YOUR BRIEFCASE IS YOUR TOOLBOX

"Every minute you spend planning saves you 10 minutes in execution; this gives you a 1,000 percent return on energy!"

Brian Tracy, Canadian-American motivational speaker and business consultant

Just like how in law you cite more than one legal case, code, or precedent, to make your point, when networking and building your practice there are multiple tools you should be using to correctly identify, engage with, and onboard prospective new clients.

Taking a myopic approach to networking your law practice will severely limit the results you are able to garner when pursuing new clientele. In sales, we use the analogy of having a robust "toolbox" of sales and business tools and knowing how and when to use them. For the purposes of this book, we are replacing the analogy of a toolbox with one of a "briefcase." Regardless, the objective is the same, which is to provide you with multiple resources, help you determine when it is appropriate to "pull them out of your briefcase," and know how to use them well.

Sidebar: Biases

As humans, our brains are hardwired to be lazy. Whenever possible, our brains will take a shortcut to reach a decision. This is because the brain only has so much energy to devote to any one particular task and, being that the brain's efforts are in constant demand, it promotes a "good-enough" decision that can be made quickly versus one that may be better, but that would require more energy to determine.[15] These shortcuts are otherwise known as biases.

We all have biases. It is part of the heuristic procedure which allows us to make quick determinations without investing the time and energy required to think carefully about every situation.[16] In most cases these biases serve us well and are helpful. However, there are times when they can negatively impact our thinking or our behavior. The first step to dealing with bias is to understand they exist and to become self-aware. By the way, our prospects and clients have biases as well. Understanding these will allow us to better navigate each interaction we have with them and to overcome any bias which may impede our ability to develop a mutually-beneficial relationship with them.

Listed below are a few common biases that you should be aware of to recognize them in your prospects, clients, and yourself.

---

[15] Psychology Today. (2022). *Bias.* Psychology Today. Retrieved Aug. 25, 2022, from https://www.psychologytoday.com/ca/basics/bias?page=0

[16] Blount, J. (2018, Jun. 13). *Objections: The Ultimate Guide for Mastering the Art and Science of Getting Past No.* Wiley.

False Consensus and Confirmation Biases

False consensus is when a person tends to overestimate the extent to which his opinions, beliefs, preferences, values, and habits are normal and typical of others. That others think as I do.[17] Confirmation bias is when we pay attention to the information that confirms our beliefs and avoid those that are contrary.[18]

Fundamental Attribution Error

This is a tendency for people to place an undue emphasis on internal characteristics (personality) to explain someone else's behavior in each situation rather than considering the situation or external factors.[19]

---

[17] Cherry, K. (2020, May 12). *How False Consensus Effect Influences the Way We Think About Others*. Very Well Mind. Retrieved from https://www.verywellmind.com/what-is-the-false-consensus-effect-2795030

[18] Cherry, K. (2021, Jul. 30). *How Confirmation Bias Works*. Very Well Mind. Retrieved from https://www.verywellmind.com/what-is-a-confirmation-bias-2795024

[19] McLeod, S. (2018). *Fundamental Attribution Error*. Simply Psychology. Retrieved from https://www.simplypsychology.org/fundamental-attribution.html

Optimism Bias

When a person believes they are at a lesser risk of experiencing a negative event.[20] An inability to recognize potential risks or hazards.

Overconfidence Bias

A person's subjective confidence in his judgment is reliably greater than the objective accuracy of those judgments.[21] Simply stated, thinking I am infallible.

Self-Enhancement Bias

The tendency for individuals to take all the credit for their success while giving little or no credit to other individuals or external forces.[22]

---

[20] Cherry, K. (2020, May 10). *Understanding the Optimism Bias: AKA the Illusion of Invulnerability*. Very Well Mind. Retrieved from https://www.verywellmind.com/what-is-the-optimism-bias-2795031

[21] Moore, D.A. (2018, Jan. 18). *Overconfidence: The Mother of All Biases. Psychology Today*. Retrieved from https://www.psychologytoday.com/ca/blog/perfectly-confident/201801/overconfidence

[22] Popova, M. (n.d.). *How Our Delusions Keep Us Sane: The Psychology of Our Essential Self-Enhancement Bias*. The Marginalian. Retrieved Jan. 26, 2022, from https://www.themarginalian.org/2014/06/04/david-mcraney-self-enchancement-bias/

Self-Serving Bias

A tendency to strengthen a person's ego by attributing positive events to his own ability and attributing negative events to forces outside his control.[23] In other words, if something good happens, I did it; if something bad happens, it is bad luck or someone else's fault.

Similarity Bias

This is when we are drawn to someone whose appearance, mannerisms, or other attributes remind us of ourselves, and we extend greater attachment and importance to them than what might be reasonable.[24]

Sunk Cost Fallacy

When an individual continues a behavior or endeavor as a result of previous investment of resources (time, money, effort).[25] They continue to pursue a course of action because

---

[23] Ruhl, C. (2021, Apr. 19). *Self-Serving Bias: Definition and Examples.* Simply Psychology. Retrieved from https://www.simplypsychology.org/self-serving-bias.html

[24] NeuroLeadership Institute. (2022, Aug.2). *The 5 Biggest Biases That Affect Decision-Making.* Your Brain At Work: NLI's Blog for all Things Neuroleadership. Retrieved Aug. 25, 2022, from https://neuroleadership.com/your-brain-at-work/seeds-model-biases-affect-decision-making/

[25] Psychology Today. (2022). *Bias.* Psychology Today. Retrieved Aug. 25, 2022, from https://www.psychologytoday.com/ca/basics/bias?page=0

of the previous investment even though the current course is not going to benefit them after all, unable to quit and try something else.

CHAPTER 9: MANAGING CLIENT RELATIONSHIPS

"The most basic human desire is to feel like you belong. Fitting in is important."

Simon Sinek, British-American leadership consultant and business advisor

Another important component of having a business development mindset is knowing how to build and leverage a network. You should constantly be creating and updating a list of contacts who are either prospective clients or who can refer you to prospective clients. The objective is to catalog the information you collect so that you can use it in the future and build upon your knowledge with each interaction. Logging the data you collect into a spreadsheet, or a customer relationship management tool will allow you to store key information so that it is easily accessible and ready to reference to help you build your contacts into meaningful and mutually-beneficial relationships.

Become familiar with the customer relationship management (CRM) tool being used by your firm. You might think that accessing the CRM is just for administrators. Think again. Another significant benefit for understanding how to use your firm's CRM system is that it allows you to share the information obtained across the firm. Now, when a client calls in, the person receiving the call can access their profile and personalize the interaction. Imagine if you had made a note about your client's birthday in the profile, and when they called in for your assistance, you wished them a happy birthday? Wouldn't that create a powerful and lasting impression?

Another advantage to sharing the information is that you encourage everyone in the firm to contribute to building your knowledge library. Having everyone participate in constantly updating your CRM is a great way to also help preserve institutional knowledge. We have heard from some that there are always one or two people who seem to know everything about a client. They can remember the name of their spouse, their favorite restaurant, how they first came to do business with the firm. They are a walking encyclopedia. What would happen if that person won the lottery and never came back to work? You would lose all that "institutional knowledge" in a millisecond. Do not compromise your data. Collect it, organize it, use it, and protect it.

While establishing a connection with someone on LinkedIn is a great start, the tool does not let you easily record notes about conversations or meetings that may be useful to reference in the future. We recommend that you look to collect information that is not readily available on a social media site like LinkedIn, to avoid duplication. This way you will maximize your time and efforts while still recording the information that is most pertinent. This information can also be useful to collect for current clients so you can develop an even deeper connection with them.

Here are a few examples of information that you may want to collect about a contact:

1. When and where you first met or who made the original introduction.

2. Current company and title or function.

3. Name of their significant other, children, or other family information.

4. Their hometown and current neighborhood.

5. Where they went to college.

6. Their favorite sport and team.

7. Common interests and hobbies.

8. Details of last conversation.

9. Potential business opportunities.

10. Introductions made or other assistance provided to each other.

Even as connections develop into partnerships or friendship you will find it useful to keep track of critical details of your relationship. This will provide you an edge in future discussions and will demonstrate your commitment to really know the people with whom you interact. This can be its own source of competitive advantage for you and your firm. You will be recognized as someone who takes relationship development seriously.

There is an adage in sales that says if you are not talking to your clients your competitors will be. It is essential to ensure consistent communication with your current clients even when they are not in immediate need of your services. You want to be talking to your clients on an ongoing basis because it is a wonderful way to show you care. And when you demonstrate that you care, you are really showing people that they are important to you. Quite frankly, people like that feeling and it works to increase their loyalty to you and your firm.

Everyone wants to feel important. Mary Kay Ash had an expression, "I imagine an invisible sign around each person's neck that says, 'Make me feel important!'" When a client hears from you when they are not in the process of utilizing your services it sends a message that you want to stay connected and your relationship with that person is important. It says I am here for you whenever you may need me, and I will do my part to ensure the lines of communication remain open. People will appreciate your sincerity and will be more likely to want to work with you and recommend you to others. You should view every relationship as a bridge to another relationship. It is a great way to stay top of mind.

For example, if you are a tax attorney, you may have a lot of interaction with clients in the months preceding the April 15th tax deadline. What if you made it a practice to contact your clients in the "off season" to simply check in with them? A few calls each week to your various clients to simply say hello and see how things are going. Inquire about their family and to see if there are any major changes on the horizon that may impact their upcoming returns. Perhaps there is a question that has been on their mind that you can easily address.

Demonstrate that you care enough to call and ask about them. They will certainly appreciate your interest and dedication to providing exceptional personalized service.

Law firms are great about being reactive. A client calls you with a need and you leap into action. However, where we often fall short is in being proactive. We fail to reach out on a consistent basis to check in and provide some unique insights. You can integrate this approach with personalized emails or by broadcasting a newsletter. While these initiatives are good, nothing beats the distinctive and personal touch of a phone call.

Remember, if they are currently your client, they like you. You are not a nuisance when you make a proactive call. You are a trusted advisor who is demonstrating you care and are committed to the relationship. It is through these efforts that you will remain top of mind and be recognized as a reliable resource when a need does arise.

Never forgo the opportunity to show you care by reaching out to your clients and prospects. You never know when your efforts will be immediately rewarded with a new opportunity. We cannot tell you the number of times we heard, "I'm so glad you called, I was just thinking of you." This will take time but will reap significant long-term rewards. You will find that persistence is a powerful tool which will allow you to grow your business significantly.

CHAPTER 10: BILLABLE HOURS

"You cannot escape the responsibility of tomorrow by evading it today."

Abraham Lincoln, American political leader and 16th President of the United States

There has been a significant amount written about time and calendar management. It is probably one of the most important skills to have a business development mindset. Here is a simple truth you need to remember: time is your most valuable resource. It is a fixed and limited resource. We have only 24 hours each day and must maximize our return on investment. It is the one thing you must manage and use wisely to ensure you are investing your time in the activities that will generate the greatest results. It is all about return on your investment. Never confuse being busy with achieving results. Everyone claims to be busy, but few can articulate what they accomplished today. Focus on accomplishing those things which will deliver the best results for your efforts and time investment.

Here is another truth. If you do not manage your time, you will discover other people are very willing to do that for you, and not always for your betterment. You will get invited to attend all kinds of meetings or events not focused on generating revenue. As Warren Buffet commented, "The difference between successful people and really successful people is that really successful people say no to almost everything." While some tasks are a part of any work environment, your ability to minimize these disruptions and work as efficiently as possible is critical. Your main job is to find, develop, and close business which generates revenue for your company and commission for you.

Do not be afraid to say "no." Let people know you respect their time, as well as your time, and find other ways to engage with and handle non-essential tasks efficiently to protect your client-facing and relationship developing time. Offer to speak to people while you are traveling to and from appointments in the car rather than coming into the office during the middle of the day. When an in-person meeting is necessary, work to schedule it early or late in the day, to preserve the central part of your day for activities that generate professional success. Always look to see what can be accomplished in an email or phone call instead of a meeting.

Use an electronic calendar which is integrated into your Customer Relationship Management (CRM) system if available. This will help you track your activities, often without having to enter activities multiple times, as well as provide members of your team easy access to your schedule. Suffice it to say that it is essential for your support team to have access to your daily planner so they know where you are and when you will be available to meet with prospects or clients. You should also understand if there are ways to integrate your phone into the CRM system for quicker updates on the go. Anything which can save you time is something you want to learn about and utilize.

There is a great deal of information available on time management. If this is an area that you find personally challenging, you may want to do some additional research or register for a class to get additional support. The information here is to provide you with some general best practices and ideas to leverage your time to maximize your results. These are proven strategies used by leading professionals to help improve and excel. You should also remember that as you develop, and you become more proficient and successful, you will want to become even more selective about where you invest your time. In the beginning, you will take appointments with semi-qualified prospects because you may have limited choices. As you build your business, you will be able to spend your time with the best prospects working on the most lucrative opportunities.

Your calendar allows you to plan and record the details of all your activities. However, you can increase the effectiveness of this tool by taking advantage of color coding your activities to provide a quick visual representation of how you are investing your time each day. You should be able to glance at your calendar and see the most important activities vividly. If you do not see the most important activities at a glance, you should stop and ask yourself what's going on. What is on your calendar other than the activities most likely to drive results? Take the appropriate action to invest your time where it will generate the greatest results. Here are some suggestions to get you started.

Green: Prospect or Client-Facing Appointments

Green is the color of money (in the United States of America). Your calendar should be filled with green if you want your pockets lined with money. You can even use two shades of green to denote the difference between an existing client meeting (dark green) and a new prospect meeting (bright green) so you can ensure a good mix of these two critical activities.

Blue: Networking Events

This includes lead-sharing group meetings, trade associations, business networking functions, as well as one-on-one meetings to cultivate relationships and foster new opportunities. Organic development of new opportunities is critical even if your firm provides you leads. You can never have too many opportunities in the works.

Yellow: Proactive Activities

You should dedicate time each week to call prospects and clients to check in and offer something of value. Too little time is dedicated to using the phone to sell.[26] It is certainly one of the most efficient ways to speak with a broad range of prospects and clients efficiently. It will allow you to uncover new information and schedule online and face-to-face appointments as appropriate. Be sure to enter important information into your CRM

---

[26] Goldfayn, A. (2021, Sept. 22). *Pick Up the Phone and Sell: How Proactive Calls to Customers and Prospects Can Double Your Sales*. Wiley.

system for future reference. Think in terms of building a strong relationship one piece of information at a time.

Orange: Mandatory Internal Meetings or Activities

These are the 'must do' items. While you cannot always control these meetings, you should work to minimize their impact on your calendar. Where possible, push back. At the very least, encourage those scheduling these activities to keep them early or late to protect the key hours of your day.

Red: Reminders

These are items with a definitive due date. When possible, use the task or 'to-do' function inside your CRM tool to capture prospect and client-related activities. Sometimes these functions can be displayed on your calendar for easy reference. This is also a great way to set reminders for submitting reports, time sheets, expenses, and anything else you are supposed to do on a regular basis which can slip your mind. Remember, these are often the little things that drive supervisors or others crazy, so stay on top of them.

Remember, this is just a suggested list. You can certainly add other colors to denote a whole host of other professional, and even personal appointments, to manage your time wisely and effectively. Most electronic calendars allow you to name the activity for each color selected. The important thing to remember is that you want to see your calendar with plenty of Green, Blue, and Yellow. These are revenue-generating activities. They should constitute the bulk of each workday. Other activities should be relegated to off hours when possible. In general, you want to keep your calendar clear from 9:00 a.m. to 4:00 p.m. to be engaged in productive engagements. Protect your time as it is your most valuable resource.

It is wonderful when you have prospects and clients who are willing to meet with you. You will certainly want to schedule as many appointments as possible. In-person visits are among the best ways to build a relationship, learn, and promote the value of your offering.

While this may appear intuitive, many professionals are so happy to get an appointment, they let the client make all the decisions about when to meet. It really is not that difficult to find some common ground if you simply ask politely. We like the idea of requesting a 'visit' for a quick chat rather than a 'meeting' for a discussion. It is a more casual way of asking to see someone face-to-face. When we visit with a networking partner, we should bring a lead, or perhaps a strategic introduction suggestion, to help our partner build their business. You get by giving. Always be willing to give first. In each of these interactions there should be a goal to improve your business. Be strategic in your thinking, so you will uncover and develop more opportunities.

CHAPTER 11: THE PEN IS MIGHTIER THAN THE SWORD

"Plan your work and work your plan."

Napoleon Hill, American author of "Think and Grow Rich"

This chapter is dedicated to sharing some tools that will help you get organized and align a business development mindset with your client acquisition efforts. Your success will depend on your ability to learn this information, practice, and then execute. There are no shortcuts. You will have to put in the time and effort to generate success. We intend to make it easier by breaking the process down into simple tasks so you can develop a rainmaker routine and the business development mindset that will take your career to the next level.

The 30-Day Action Plan

This plan is designed to give you practical guidance on starting the process. It outlines activities that should take just a few minutes per day to get your business development efforts going in the right direction. We highly recommend that you put this information on your calendar as a daily reminder of the tasks to complete. You will discover that as you work your plan you will see incremental improvements in both your performance and your results. Persistence will be your guiding principle to achieve long term success.

Week 1: Initial Preparation & Personal Brand Review

- LinkedIn Profile Review and Update
- Other Social Media Profile Updates

Develop Ideal Client Profile

- Who would be an ideal new client for my practice? For the firm?

Speak with Current Clients

- Who might they know to make an introduction?
- Are there any other opportunities for the firm to be of service? (Other practice areas).

Week 2: Research and Planning

- Warm Introductions – Leverage LinkedIn
    - Who do I know who may know someone who is a potential ideal client?

    - Identify a list of those friends and associates who can make strategic introductions with the name of the person you want to meet.
- Set aside time on your calendar to make phone calls to associates to request their assistance and to send follow-up emails.
- Social Media Content – Developing Subject Matter Expertise
    - What do you have to share that would be of value? What is going on in your area of expertise that might be of interest to others?
    - What information can you share that has been posted by other sources such as associations or other experts?
- Select Association / Networking Groups to Participate
    - Review upcoming events and put them on the calendar.
    - Send an email to the Membership Chairperson to express interest in joining; confirm you can attend the next event to "check it out."

Week 3: Implementation

- Begin Making Proactive Phone Calls
    - Talk to Clients
    - Ask Associates for Warm Introductions
    - Send Out Introductory Emails
    - Schedule Times to "Chat" Virtually or In Person
- Post Information on LinkedIn
    - Share Relevant Information Weekly
    - Review and Comment on Other People's Posts
    - Search for Potential Connections and Send Personalized Note to Connect

While LinkedIn provides you the opportunity to send a connection request without any personalization, a best practice is for you to utilize the "Personal Note" option. We have found that when you take a moment to personalize the invitation the likelihood of securing the connection increases dramatically. It should be both brief and simple. Here are a couple of examples:

Hello Chris, I noticed your posting about "something" this morning. We share a common interest in this topic. Thought it would be nice to connect. Thank you. Bob

Hello Julie, I read your article about "something" and found your approach both unique and compelling. Thought it would be nice to connect with you. Thank you. Vince

Week 4: Follow Up and Next Steps

- Follow Up on Invitations Sent and Introductions Made
  - Start the conversation and keep it going.
- LinkedIn Postings
  - How many views and shares did your first post generate?
  - Have you received any new invitations to connect?
  - What will you share next? Make sure it is on the calendar.
- Evaluate and Adjust

- What's working?
- What needs more attention?
- What can you do next?
- Obtain your Social Selling Index Score (SSI) weekly.

Depending on the size of your firm, and their commitment to business development, you may have a Marketing Team on staff. Their responsibilities may include developing brochures, assisting with presentations, and attending industry events to promote the firm. If you are fortunate enough to have one or more marketing professionals available to assist you, we recommend that you immediately schedule a time to meet with them. We suggest a lunch meeting to review their skills, specialties, and ability to help you develop a sales mindset and promote your practice. We think you will find that they are willing to support your efforts. To be honest, they have probably been preaching the benefits of all the items discussed in this book. Now is the time to get some personalized support and engage an "accountability partner" who can help you implement these ideas and generate the results you desire.

If you don't have access to a professional marketing team, you may find it helpful to find someone else either in your firm, or another attorney you know, to help you stay the course. It is always nice to have someone to share ideas and preview your activities to make suggestions or comments so you can present your best efforts.

In some circumstances, hiring a professional coach (like the authors of this book) to assist you with developing your personal brand and taking the necessary steps to promote yourself and begin developing a sales or business development mindset might be a worthy investment. Nearly every well-known athlete has a coach to help them develop their talents to the fullest while learning new skills to remain competitive. It might help you jump start your efforts as well.

SECTION 5: SUMMATION

"The dollar bills the customer gets from tellers in four banks are the same. What is different are the tellers."

Stanley Marcus, American retailer and chairman of luxury department store, Neiman Marcus

We are nearing the end of this book. We hope you found our case for developing a business development mindset compelling and recognize the benefits you can realize by incorporating this new skill into your repertoire. Whether you are a solo practitioner or a member of a large firm, the ability to attract, develop, and retain clients is essential. Depending on your specific circumstances it could mean the difference between success, mediocrity, or failure.

While we are coming to the end of this book, we have not necessarily reached the end of our journey together. We will continue to be a resource to you through our website at www.imnotinsales.com. You will be able to access additional resources and information to support your efforts as well as learn from other attorneys about their journey. You will also be able to email us with questions or schedule time to chat if that would be helpful. We appreciate your attention and willingness to promote your business development mindset.

Sidebar: Business Development Habits for Success

This is the final section and you have taken an important first step toward becoming proficient at business development by this book. Now that you have learned the fundamentals, it is time to put these new skills into practice. Develop the habits that will make it easier to utilize these new skills going forward and help you achieve the results you desire.

We want to take a few moments to discuss the word "habit." Too often we refer to a habit when it has a negative connotation, as in a "bad habit," because of the negative impact. However, "good habits" are formed the same way. In some cases, habits are formed without a thoughtful intention. It just becomes an automatic action given our past experiences. In this case, we are looking to proactively form a good habit. Experts debate the actual length of time it takes to form a habit, but at a minimum it takes 21 days of repeated activity and positive reinforcement. In short, it requires you to commit and act daily to achieve continuous improvement and realize the benefits of a business development mindset.

Who knows, you may become so good at this you earn the moniker "rainmaker" at your firm and achieve greater heights than you ever thought possible.

> Imagine combining your stellar legal prowess with your newly developed client acquisition talents!

In this book, Vince and I have shown you the tools you will need to have a sales mindset and demonstrated how to use them. After completing this book, you now have a full briefcase of tools to help you grow your legal practice.

The best advice we can give you is to not try and do everything at once. We don't want you to overwhelm yourself. Rather, pick three things that you can do now against which you can measure results. My suggestion is to start with your LinkedIn profile. Post a professional headshot and create a meaningful job description and value statement of why clients should hire you. Next, use LinkedIn to identify prospective clients so you can interact with them by liking their posts and commenting on them. Once you've established some rapport, reach out to connect with them to learn more about them and where they may need legal assistance. It's really as simple as having a conversation.

The good news is that your learning does not stop with this book. Use this book as a catalyst to garner more knowledge. We encourage you to consume as many resources as possible to help you in your journey to achieve a sales mindset and to grow your legal practice.

Of course, if you and your law firm are interested, Vince and I can discuss what it would look like for us to deliver a customized and personalized training program.

We wish you success in becoming not just a great lawyer, but a financially successful one as well.

CHAPTER 12: CLOSING ARGUMENT

"Get closer than ever to your customers. So close that you tell them what they need well before they realize it themselves."

Steve Jobs, American entrepreneur, inventor, and co-founder of Apple, Inc.

A good lawyer must have a business development mindset that includes at least two basic qualities: ego drive and empathy. This mindset is what propels lawyers to the pinnacle of their profession. Here are some easy-to-follow suggestions, inspired by top legal rainmakers, so you too can build a business development mindset.

- They don't think in terms of acquiring a client, but rather in terms of building a relationship.

- They build their businesses one client at a time and then leverage the last client for referrals to get their next client.

- They listen more than they speak, gaining an understanding of the client's needs to help find a resolution.

- They deliver more than they promise, and always promise a great deal!

- They invest their time in things (people) that positively affect their income and avoid spending time on things (people) that have no return.

- They are always seeking new, better, and faster ways to increase their ability to retain more clients.

- They're willing to invest in networking, community, and relationships, knowing that the difference between a contact and a contract is the "R" and it stands for "Relationship."

- They are masters of their own destinies and don't depend on marketplace economies for their outcomes. They instead rely on their own actions.

- They surround themselves with overachievers and have little time for those who don't create opportunities.

- They never accept good enough as good enough.

- They don't see failed attempts to retain clients as failures but as investments in their process.

- They never give up on unretained clients, knowing that someday those clients will either need them or refer them.

- They squeeze hours out of minutes and weeks out of days.

- They see problems as opportunities.
- They continually invest in their education, development, and personal motivation, knowing that these are the tools of a consummate legal professional.
- They invest in their careers, their businesses, and their clients.
- They hold themselves to performance standards that are higher than even those of their managing partners.
- They don't need others to hold them accountable.
- They are constantly in think, plan, and prepare mode in order to continue to build their client base and keep their pipelines full.
- They take the time to visualize their future and then to put in place the concrete steps it will take to get there.

ACKNOWLEDGEMENTS

We would like to take this opportunity to thank those who have contributed to the creation of this work.

Arthur Uratani, Director of Marketing and Outreach for Bookoff McAndrews PLLC located in Washington, DC: Arthur has nearly 19 years of experience marketing legal services for prestigious firms as well as being a leader in the nationally recognized Legal Marketing Association. Thank you, Arthur, for your friendship and your early reading of this book. Your insights and suggestions enabled us to fine tune our approach to create a compelling story for attorneys interested in developing a business development mindset.

Dawn E. Boyce, Principal and Managing Partner at McGavin, Boyce, Bardot, Thorsen & Katz, PC located in Fairfax, Virginia: Dawn has extensive experience as an attorney and leader. Her review of an early edition of the book provided us fantastic insights into what partners expect from their associates when it comes to attracting new clients and the importance of cultivating a business development mindset.

ABOUT THE AUTHORS

Bob Greene is an accomplished and nationally recognized corporate sales trainer and strategic business advisor. As CEO of RCGWorkgroup.com, he provides tailored solutions to companies of all sizes, from Fortune 500 to start-ups, helping to meet and exceed the unique business needs of each client. Bob is the 2023 Institute for Excellence in Sales Member of the Year, an adjunct faculty member for sales leadership with the American Management Association, a leadership trainer for the Federal Government and US Military, and a frequent commentator on business advancement strategies.

Bob holds a degree in Political Science and Organizational Leadership from Virginia Tech, a BMI Certificate in Intercultural Analysis, and an Executive Certificate in Strategic Negotiation from the MIT Sloan School of Management. In his personal life, Bob is a father of five and lives in Northern Virginia with his wife and two of his teenage sons.

Vincent D. Burruano received his MBA in Business Administration, Management and Operations from The

George Washington University and his Bachelor of Philosophy from the School of Philosophy at the Catholic University of America, both located in Washington, DC. He was most recently Vice President of Sales for the Commercial Division of JK Moving Services, one of the nation's largest independent movers, in Sterling, Virginia. Vince is the 2022 Institute for Excellence in Sales Member of the Year. Today, he operates his own consulting business, Vince Burruano Consulting Services, LLC in Summerville, South Carolina. Vince believes that learning and growth are the key to success at both the individual and team levels.

In his spare time, Vince is an avid reader and enjoys traveling. He has been a volunteer first responder and firefighter, a football and baseball coach, served on the Board of Directors and Executive Sales Leadership Team with the Office Moving Alliance, and is a Member of the Lido Civic Club of Washington, DC and Rotary International. Vince also serves as a Forbes Business Development Council Member, writing articles for their members. Vince is a published author of *A Daily Dose of Sales Wisdom: Practical Advice for Sales Professionals and Leaders to Excel* and *The New Sales*

Professional's Playbook: Jumpstart Your Sales Career Today.

Vince resides in Summerville, South Carolina with his wife, Elizabeth, his son, Michael, daughter-in-law, Meghan, and granddaughter, Shaylin, and members of their extended family live nearby.

REVIEWS

"Vince and Bob understand that many attorneys believe their work and reputations sell themselves, but in a day of ever-changing personnel, company structures, and work environment, they also understand more is needed. We, as attorneys, need to listen, engage, and connect to build our practices and develop our businesses. This book is an excellent way to learn how."

Dawn E. Boyce, McGavin, Boyce, Bardot, Thorsen & Katz, P.C.

"Vince and Bob are fantastic at explaining why and how a business development mindset can immensely benefit lawyers. What I love about their book is they give us an easy-to-read, best practices manual filled with actionable items, relatable scenarios, mind-blowing statistics, and fantastic bits of wisdom (and quotes!). I plan on coming back to read this over and over again for inspiration!"

Arthur Uratani, Director of Marketing and Outreach for Bookoff McAndrews PLLC & President-Elect of the Mid-Atlantic Region, Legal Marketing Association

APPENDIX A: SUGGESTED RESOURCES & BOOKS

While we hope you found this book to be informative and useful in helping you cultivate a sales mindset to enhance your business development efforts, we would be remiss not to identify the many other authors and experts on the subject. Listed below are just a few of the many resources available that will help you take your efforts to the next level.

Blanchard, K.H., & Bowles, S.M. (1993). *Raving Fans: A Revolutionary Approach to Customer Service.* William Morrow.

Blount, J. (2018, Jun. 13). *Objections: The Ultimate Guide for Mastering the Art and Science of Getting Past No.* Wiley.

Blount, J. (2010, Jun. 21). *People Buy You: The Real Secret to What Matters Most in Business.* Wiley.

Blount, J. (2017, Mar. 20). *Sales EQ: How Ultra High Performers Leverage Sales-Specific Emotional Intelligence to Close the Complex Deal.* Wiley.

Davis, K. (1996). *Getting into Your Customer's Head: 8 Secret Roles of Selling Your Competitors Don't Know.* Crown Business.

Goldfayn, A. (2021, Sept. 22). *Pick Up the Phone and Sell: How Proactive Calls to Customers and Prospects Can Double Your Sales.* Wiley.

Hunter, M. (2016). *High-Profit Prospecting: Powerful Strategies to Find the Best Leads and Drive Breakthrough Sales Results.* AMACOM.

Kelly, M.C. (2011). *15 Ways to Grow Your Business In Every Economy.* Productive Leaders.

Levick, R., with Slack, C. (2010). *The Communicators: Leadership In the Age of Crisis.* Watershed Press.

Loehr, J. (2008). *The Power of Story: Change Your Story, Change Your Destiny in Business and in Life.* Free Press.

Schroeder, A. (2009). *The Snowball: Warren Buffett and the Business of Life.* Bantam.

Weinberg, M. (2012, Sept. 4). *New Sales. Simplified: The Essential Handbook for Prospecting and New Business Development.* AMACOM.

Weiss, A. (2021, Jun. 22). *The Consulting Bible: How to Launch and Grow a Seven-Figure Consulting*

APPENDIX B: PROFESSIONAL ORGANIZATIONS

American Academy of Forensic Sciences (AAFS) is a membership organization that provides leadership to advance science and its application to the legal system (aafs.org).

American Association for Justice (AAJ) provides lawyers with the information and professional assistance needed to serve clients successfully and protect the democratic values inherent in the civil justice system (justice.org).

American Bar Association (ABA) is a membership organization for practicing attorneys, in-house lawyers, legal professionals, law students, and provides resources on a wealth of issues addressing bias, racism and prejudice in the justice system and society among other areas (americanbar.org).	
American Health Lawyers Association (AHLA) is the nation's largest, nonpartisan educational organization devoted to legal issues in the healthcare field (healthlawyers.org).	
American Immigration Lawyers Association (AILA) advances the quality of immigration and nationality law and practice and enhance the professional development of its	

members (aila.org).	
Association of Corporate Counsel (ACC) is the world's largest organization dedicated to in-house counsel (acc.com).	
Association of Eminent Domain Professionals (AEDP) is an organization of professionals in a variety of disciplines specializing in the field of eminent domain (aedp.org).	
Association of Legal Administrators (ALA) is the undisputed leader in the business of law and law practice management (alanet.org).	

Association of Prosecuting Attorneys (APA) provides valuable training and technical assistance to prosecutors to develop proactive and innovative prosecutorial practices (apainc.org).	
Business Network International (BNI) is the world's leading business referral organization with over 291,714 Members in over 10,800 BNI Chapters worldwide (bni.com).	
Chicago Women in Intellectual Property (ChiWIP) is a networking and mentoring organization committed to the connection, promotion, and success of Chicagoland area women in the intellectual property law field (chiwip.org).	

Kiwanis International is a global community of clubs, members and partners dedicated to improving the lives of children one community at a time (kiwanis.org).	
Lifehack started as a blog featuring resources and tips for better productivity and lifestyle. Now it features How To Start and Run a Mastermind Group (lifehack.org).	
National Association for Legal Professionals (NALS) is a leader in the legal services industry (nals.org).	
National Association of Attorneys General (NAAG) helps attorneys general fulfill the responsibilities of their office and to assist in the delivery of high-	

quality legal services (naag.org).	
National Association of Consumer Advocates (NACA) is a nationwide organization of more than 1,500 attorneys who represent and have represented hundreds of thousands of consumers (consumeradvocates.org).	
National Association of Criminal Defense Lawyers (NACDL) is the preeminent organization in the United States advancing the mission of the nation's criminal defense lawyers (nacdl.org).	
National Association of Hearing Officials (NAHO) is a membership organization comprised of individuals involved in the process of administrative	

adjudication (naho.org).	
National Association of Legal Investigators (NALI) is a membership organization for legal investigators actively engaged in negligence investigations for the plaintiff and/or criminal defense (nalionline.org).	
National Association of Patent Practitioners (NAPP) is dedicated to supporting patent practitioners and those working in the field of patent law (napp.org).	
National Association of Subrogation Professionals (NASP) enhances the stature and effectiveness of subrogation and recovery professionals (subrogation.org).	

National Conference of Black Lawyers (NCBL) is an association of lawyers, scholars, judges, legal workers, law students, and legal activists. We exist for the purpose of enhancing our professional strength and skill for the benefit of the Black community in its struggle for full social, political, and economic rights. We seek to utilize the vehicles of the law to advance the fight against racism (white supremacy) and the inequities it produces (ncbl.org).	
National Employment Lawyers Association (NELA) advances employee rights and serves lawyers who advocate for equality and justice in the American workplace (nela.org).	

Optimist International is a worldwide volunteer organization made up of more than 2,500 local Clubs whose Members work each day to make the future brighter by bringing out the best in children, in their communities, and in themselves (optimist.org).	
Professional Networking Association Northwest (PNANW) is the fastest growing business networking organization in the Pacific Northwest (pnanw.com).	
Rotary International is a global network of 1.4 million neighbors, friends, leaders, and problem-solvers who see a world where people unite and take action to create lasting change across the globe, in our communities, and in ourselves	

(rotary.org).	
SCORE is the nation's largest network of volunteer, expert business mentors, and is dedicated to helping small businesses get off the ground, grow and achieve their goals (score.org).	
Leadership Council on Legal Diversity (LCLD) was founded in 2009 and has grown to an organization of more than 400 Members, who serve as either general counsel of major corporations or managing partners of the nation's leading law firms. United by a spirit of activism and personal commitment, LCLD Members participate widely in the programs they've created—leading by example, taking action, and challenging the legal profession to prepare future generations of	

diverse talent for the highest positions of leadership (lcldnet.org).	
Women in Business & Industry - Women Helping Build Their Communities Through Entrepreneurial Work (wib-i.com).	
U.S. Chamber of Commerce | Standing Up for American Enterprise: the world's largest business organization (uschamber.com).	
YPO Young Professionals Organization is the global leadership community of extraordinary chief executives (ypo.org).	

APPENDIX C: GLOSSARY

Benefits: Are those things a client realizes from being represented by you. Benefits can be both "hard" and "soft." For example, a hard benefit is saving money while a soft benefit is finding you easy to engage. Benefits are what people want when they purchase a product or service. There is an old saying that people do not buy a drill because they want a drill, they buy a drill because they want holes. They are purchasing the benefits offered, in this case the ability to create holes. While your solution may offer a range of benefits, only the prospect can determine which benefit is of value to them for their specific situation. Benefits are personal to each client and create the emotional need to decide.

Business Development: Is the art of cultivating relationships that will lead to business opportunities. We make a distinction between "selling" and "business development" but will occasionally use the terms interchangeably.

Buyer's Remorse: A situation where the person who purchased a product or service now feels remorse for making that decision. It is a psychological state where the person regrets their decision for one or more of several factors. This may include unmet expectations, a lack of fulfillment, a feeling of betrayal, or paying too much. This situation is part of the fear most people have when having to decide and is often why the status quo is preferred to the risk of change.

Coach: A person inside or outside the prospective target organization that can provide you insights and guidance in your pursuit of a business opportunity. This role is key especially in larger organizations or strategic accounts where there are multiple players or levels of decision-making authority. A coach can provide you direction and advice about the players, the process, the culture, and other factors that will influence how to proceed. The coach can also provide you feedback on your progress and potential competitors or challenges to your attempt to secure new business. It is essential to identify and cultivate coaches in the companies you are targeting. Even if you are dealing with the most senior executives, a coach can provide you insights that will allow you to navigate the decision-making process.

Cold Call: A cold call is when you make an unsolicited call on a potential suspect in hopes of engaging them in conversation and to cultivate them into a prospect. Cold calling is one of the most difficult skills to master and has the lowest probability of converting suspects into new business. However, if you are unable to cultivate relationships using other methods you may have to resort to this type of activity. The good news is that there are ways to "warm up" a cold call to improve the chances of engagement. We spend time discussing this throughout the book.

Competitive Advantage: The difference between you and your firm when compared to those offering similar services to a prospective client. It is essential to understand what makes you and your company unique and different so that you can cultivate that distinction in the mind of the prospect. It is important to realize that being unique or different is only an advantage if the prospect recognizes the value that creates for him or his company. Just because you offer a difference does not mean that it necessarily creates value for the prospect. All other things being equal, the only factor remaining is price. For example, why would you spend more money when purchasing a legal pad from Company A when Company B offered the identical item for less? You never want price to be the determining factor unless you are the low-price leader in a market or industry. While we do not provide you guidance for pricing your services in this book, we can certainly encourage you to understand the value you create for a client and set your prices accordingly. The more value you create the more benefits are realized. This may allow you to charge a premium price for the services you offer. It is important to remember that you are part of the value formula. You are unique and different and will bring value to the prospect. Remember that is an essential part of your offering and be sure to cultivate that value for your prospect.

Customer Experience: As known as CX. Simply put, how you make a prospect or client want to do business with you and your firm. Now more than ever, leveraging someone's feelings is critical to securing them as a long-term client. It begins with their first engagement with you, including the advertising and marketing material you promote, through the initial connection and discussion, all the way through the sale and the processing of the invoice. People have certain expectations about how they will be treated and how they will feel doing business with you. If those expectations are not met or are otherwise compromised the opportunity for buyer's remorse can set in. The person will begin to question their decision to engage you and may decide to terminate further business with you and your firm.

Customer Relationship Management (CRM): This can refer to both the process of managing your ongoing relationships as well as the software (Salesforce.com, HubSpot, etc.) used to track prospects and clients. There are other software tools especially for law firms that incorporate CRM capabilities with other functions related to the firm's operations including time tracking and case management. We dedicate a full chapter to exploring this important concept and encourage you to evaluate which option might be best for you. You may find that your current systems can easily be upgraded to incorporate a CRM component as compared to making a new investment.

Decision Influencer: A person or persons in an organization that will provide input and influence a decision to purchase a product or service. While a decision influencer may not have the authority to say "yes" they often have the power to say "no."

Decision-Maker: The ultimate authority that will decide on your proposal or recommendation. While this may be a single individual, it is now often a collection of people either working linearly or collectively. It is critical to understand the decision-making process when you engage with a prospect. It may be the person you are working with is fully authorized to make the decision to hire you, or they may need to consult another person or group to make a final decision. Learning who is involved will help you understand their needs and concerns to best position yourself to earn their business.

Differentiation: What separates you from your competition. You should be able to clearly articulate the differences you and your firm can offer, which can include a host of variables such as ease of doing business, capabilities offered, expertise and experience, past performance, and customer experience. Differentiation helps to answer the question, "Why should I do business with you?" The more clear and powerful the answer, the more likely you will be able to win business over from your competitors. Lee B. Salz, aka the Sales Architect, has done fantastic work exploring this concept and its importance in his book Sales Differentiation. We highly recommend you add it to your library.

Explicit Needs: When a suspect can articulate a specific problem or challenge that needs to be addressed, including a desire to evaluate options and find a solution. The suspect has mentally acknowledged they have an issue they want to have resolved. They are in the "I need this or want that" mode of thinking. Again, using our car driver as an example, they lost control of their car on a rain-soaked road and ran into the back of another car, and caused injuries. They now need legal representation to protect them against litigation.

Ideal Client Profile (ICP): Is how you describe your best clients and where to find them. ICP's have challenges that you can address well and create substantial benefits for. Using an ICP is a proven way to identify the type of prospects you should be pursuing to give you the best opportunity to secure new business for yourself and your firm.

Ideally-Qualified Prospect (IQP): An ideally qualified prospect represents the perfect situation for what you offer. Their needs align well with what you have to offer. You can easily address their problems and offer a great solution that will create value for them. Your capabilities are a perfect match for their challenges. They will see significant value in what you offer and are willing to pay top dollar to obtain those benefits. It is the client that you would want to do business with every day.

Influencer: An influencer is someone in an organization, or associated with the company, who cannot decide on their own to do business with you, but has access to the decision-making authority, understands the politics and players, and can exert some degree of pressure to get your offering considered. An influencer can often function as a coach who can help you navigate the corporate landscape to win the business.

Implicit Needs: These needs lay under the surface and need to be nurtured into explicit needs to motivate action. If you would like, think of someone with an implicit need as a driver on a dark rainy night…before they get into a car accident.

Lead: A lead is when you are provided key information about a prospect who has expressed interest in the services you provide. Leads come in a variety of formats. They can be a request from your company website by a person looking for additional information or an opportunity provided to you from a colleague or networking partner. A lead is an excellent way to identify someone who has a need that you can address.

There are various levels of leads depending on the timeframe for a decision. For example, a “cold lead” is equivalent to a suspect while a “hot lead” is someone actively investigating solutions to make an imminent decision. It is critically important that you follow up on all leads immediately to qualify their status and engage the prospect.

Lead or Referral Group: A Lead or Referral Group is an organized team that meets on a regular basis to share information about potential prospects and to make warm introductions. An example is Business Networking International (BNI). Participants represent various industries calling on the same target audience. Most groups will also limit participation to one of each type of service provider to eliminate internal competition. These groups offer an excellent opportunity to identify potential prospects as well as leverage the group’s combined list of connections. Often a leads group is a fantastic way to receive warm introductions to complimentary connections that can grow your personal network.

Open and Closed Ended Questions: Questions are the foundation to learning about other people. There is an adage that says, "You have two ears and one mouth. Listen twice as much as you speak." You learn the most and best when you are listening. Just like in litigation, the person asking the questions drives the conversation. It is important to understand the difference between these diverse types of questions and how to use them most effectively during a conversation. Open-ended questions are those questions that cannot be answered with a simple yes or no response. They require greater clarification and encourage someone to share more details about a topic. Examples include, "Tell me about the last time you considered hiring a lawyer?" or "What was your experience the last time you looked for an attorney to address a legal matter for you?" These questions will encourage the person to share both facts and feelings about their experiences which will allow you to ask more targeted follow up questions to better understand their specific situation. A closed-ended question is one that can be simply answered with a brief response. It solicits a yes or no confirmation or a fact such as a number. For example, "How many times a year do you engage an attorney?" or "Are you currently represented by counsel?" The purpose is to get a fact so that you may then follow up with an open-ended question to further explore a topic. It is also an effective way to summarize or confirm your understanding of the information that has been provided. For example, you may ask "What you're saying is that now that your business is growing rapidly and exposed to greater liability, you require the services of a law firm to help you mitigate risk, correct?" This question succinctly confirms the facts and allows you to continue the discussion.

Pipeline: Pipeline refers to the qualified prospects you are working with to onboard as clients. It is also referred to as your qualified opportunities. It will denote the name of the prospect, the type of service they need, the potential amount of the contract or engagement, and the estimated timeline for when a decision will be made. This is a great tool to manage your known sales opportunities. A pipeline is an essential tool for managing your future business. If you cannot identify upcoming business opportunities, you will find yourself with sufficient opportunities to be a going concern. A well-qualified pipeline is essential to any business. We have provided examples at http://www.imnotinsales.com for your review and utilization.

Prospect: A prospect is a person who has a need you can fulfill. They are actively looking for a solution to a problem and may want to purchase your service. They will be looking for options to address their issue to select a solution. Prospects are aware of their basic needs and have indicated some level of interest in resolving their needs. These are people looking to make a decision.

Qualification Process: This refers to the process of questioning a suspect to uncover their potential needs and how you or your firm can address those needs. It is the first step in converting a suspect into a prospect. This process involves converting implicit needs into explicit needs by asking open-ended questions to draw out what the prospect wants and expects. It is essential to qualify every prospect before you invest time in developing a potential recommendation. Not everyone is your ideal prospect. The qualification process will allow you to discern if they have needs that you can satisfy and if there will be sufficient value created for them to want to pay for your services. There is nothing worse than spending time with someone who does not have a problem you can solve or the authority to purchase or recommend your offering.

Referral: A referral is when someone introduces you to a prospect and offers their personal recommendation to do business with you. It is an extension of the trust a person has for you and your company. It is a powerful tool to generate new business. It is also the thing you most want from your friends, clients, and associates. A referral can be the shortest distance between a prospect and a new client.

Sales Process: The sales process is a straightforward way of understanding the steps involved in transforming a suspect into a customer. Every law firm should develop its own sales process to include the steps required. The visual represents the typical steps in a sales process.

1. Suspect
2. Prospect
3. Qualify
4. Demonstrate
5. Recommend
6. Negotiate
7. Decision

It is important to recognize that each step has several sub-steps that need to be completed before moving to the next phase. Of import is that every sales process has the same elements of being measurable, repeatable, and sustainable. The power of this tool is that it provides you with a clear path for developing opportunities and migrating them into new business. We highly recommend that you articulate, in writing, your specific process and update it accordingly.

Selling: Is the art of getting someone to purchase a product or service. It involves active promotion of your product or service to potential customers. It may involve a simple transaction, a one-time purchase, or an effort to secure an ongoing relationship where the purchasing activity occurs repeatedly over time.

Suspect: A suspect is someone who may need your service. They fit the typical profile of a buyer but currently do not have a specific need or an expressed interest. In this state they are not actively looking for your services but have the profile of someone who often needs your services. A suspect becomes a prospect once they recognize their need for what you offer.

Target Audience: Your target audience is the ideal set of prospects that you want to engage. They are the ones most likely to need and benefit from your services. In short, it is a collection of your ideal prospects who most desire to engage.

Warm Introduction: When a person introduces you to someone they know and provides a personal recommendation that says they should speak with you. You can receive a warm introduction to a suspect or prospect as well as to a potential networking partner. This is an essential way to increase your sphere of influence and build new relationships.

Made in the USA
Monee, IL
13 September 2026

62981969R00115